MW00437564

George A. Charalampidis

PLATO'S REPUBLIC: THE MYTH OF ER

An unconventional interpretation
of the Universe in the first description
of an out-of-body experience
in *Plato's Republic*

Àκακία
PUBLICATIONS

GEORGE A. CHARALAMPIDIS

PLATO'S REPUBLIC:
THE MYTH OF ER

An unconventional interpretation
of the Universe in the first description
of an out-of-body experience
in *Plato's Republic*

ISBN: 978-1-911352-68-6

Cover Image:
Source: ShutterStock.com / Copyright: Anastasios71 / File No: 178850363
Mixed and Designed by AKAKIA Publications

Translation: Dr. Vassilios N. Manimanis

ΑκΑκία
PUBLICATIONS

19 Ashmead, Chase Road,N14 4QX, London, UK
T. 0044 207 1244 057
F. 0044 203 4325 030

www.akakia.net
publications@akakia.net

2016, London, UK

This book is dedicated to my mother.

CONTENTS

The ancient text 9

Preface 21

INTERPRETATION OF THE ANCIENT TEXT 27

Chapter 1
THE SECRET IDENTITY OF ER 29

Chapter 2
DESCRIBING THE ROUTE OF THE SOUL OF ER IN THE
INVISIBLE WORLD 57

Chapter 3
THE MYTH OF ANDROGYNOUS HUMANS AND THE
HOLY FESTIVAL 81

Chapter 4
THE SUM OF THE KARMA OF OUR SOULS 95

Chapter 5
THE CASE OF ARDIAEUS THE TYRANT 107

Chapter 6
A PLATONIC DESCRIPTION OF THE UNIVERSE 119

Chapter 7
THE SPINDLE OF NECESSITY 131

Chapter 8
A DESCRIPTION OF THE PLANETS AND THE KNEE
OF NECESSITY 151

Chapter 9
THE THREE FATES 171

Chapter 10
A "CONTRACT OF REINCARNATION"................................ 185

Chapter 11
THE PROCESS OF SELECTING THE NEXT
REINCARNATION 195

Chapter 12
THE GRANDEUR OF THE FREE WILL............................. 209

Chapter 13
GUIDELINES TO TRAVELLERS 219

Chapter 14
THE UNIQUE VALUE OF PHILOSOPHY
AND OF THE FREE WILL... 229

Chapter 15
THE UNKNOWN SECRETS OF METEMPSYCHOSIS
AND REINCARNATIONS... 239

Chapter 16
THE DAEMON OR GUARDIAN ANGEL
AND THE FUNCTION OF THE THREE FATES 255

Chapter 17
AFTERWORD — THE SALVATION OF THE SOUL........ 269

BIBLIOGRAPHY 275

About the author... 277

The ancient text

Chapter 1

ἀλλ' οὐ μέντοι σοι, ἦν δ' ἐγώ, Ἀλκίνου γε ἀπόλογον ἐρῶ, ἀλλ' ἀλκίμου μὲν ἀνδρός, Ἡρὸς τοῦ Ἀρμενίου, τὸ γένος Παμφύλου· ὅς ποτε ἐν πολέμῳ τελευτήσας, ἀναιρεθέντων δεκαταίων τῶν νεκρῶν ἤδη διεφθαρμένων, ὑγιὴς μὲν ἀνῃρέθη, κομισθεὶς δ' οἴκαδε μέλλων θάπτεσθαι δωδεκαταῖος ἐπὶ τῇ πυρᾷ κείμενος ἀνεβίω, ἀναβιοὺς δ' ἔλεγεν ἃ ἐκεῖ ἴδοι.

Chapter 2

ἔφη δέ, ἐπειδὴ οὗ ἐκβῆναι, τὴν ψυχὴν πορεύεσθαι [614c] μετὰ πολλῶν, καὶ ἀφικνεῖσθαι σφᾶς εἰς τόπον τινὰ δαιμόνιον, ἐν ᾧ τῆς τε γῆς δύ' εἶναι χάσματα ἐχομένω ἀλλήλοιν καὶ τοῦ οὐρανοῦ αὖ ἐν τῷ ἄνω ἄλλα καταντικρύ. δικαστὰς δὲ μεταξὺ τούτων καθῆσθαι, οὕς, ἐπειδὴ διαδικάσειαν, τοὺς μὲν δικαίους κελεύειν πορεύεσθαι τὴν εἰς δεξιάν τε καὶ ἄνω διὰ τοῦ οὐρανοῦ, σημεῖα περιάψαντας τῶν δεδικασμένων ἐν τῷ πρόσθεν, τοὺς δὲ ἀδίκους τὴν εἰς ἀριστεράν τε καὶ κάτω, ἔχοντας καὶ τούτους ἐν τῷ ὄπισθεν σημεῖα πάντων ὧν [614d] ἔπραξαν. ἑαυτοῦ δὲ προσελθόντος εἰπεῖν ὅτι δέοι αὐτὸν ἄγγελον ἀνθρώποις γενέσθαι τῶν ἐκεῖ καὶ διακελεύοιντό οἱ ἀκούειν τε καὶ θεᾶσθαι πάντα τὰ ἐν τῷ τόπῳ. ὁρᾶν δὴ ταύτῃ μὲν καθ' ἑκάτερον τὸ χάσμα τοῦ οὐρανοῦ τε καὶ τῆς γῆς ἀπιούσας τὰς ψυχάς, ἐπειδὴ αὐταῖς δικασθείη, κατὰ δὲ τὼ ἑτέρω ἐκ μὲν τοῦ ἀνιέναι ἐκ τῆς γῆς μεστὰς αὔχμοῦ τε καὶ κόνεως, ἐκ δὲ τοῦ ἑτέρου καταβαίνειν ἑτέρας ἐκ τοῦ [614e] οὐρανοῦ καθαράς.

Chapter 3

καὶ τὰς ἀεὶ ἀφικνουμένας ὥσπερ ἐκ πολλῆς πορείας φαίνεσθαι ἥκειν, καὶ ἀσμένας εἰς τὸν λειμῶνα ἀπιούσας οἷον ἐν πανηγύρει κατασκηνᾶσθαι, καὶ ἀσπάζεσθαί τε ἀλλήλας ὅσαι γνώριμαι, καὶ πυνθάνεσθαι τάς τε ἐκ τῆς γῆς ἡκούσας παρὰ τῶν ἑτέρων τὰ ἐκεῖ καὶ τὰς ἐκ τοῦ οὐρανοῦ τὰ παρ' ἐκείναις. διηγεῖσθαι δὲ ἀλλήλαις τὰς [615a] μὲν ὀδυρομένας τε καὶ κλαούσας, ἀναμιμνησκομένας ὅσα τε καὶ οἷα πάθοιεν καὶ ἴδοιεν ἐν τῇ ὑπὸ γῆς πορείᾳ-εἶναι δὲ τὴν πορείαν χιλιέτη-τὰς δ' αὖ ἐκ τοῦ οὐρανοῦ εὐπαθείας διηγεῖσθαι καὶ θέας ἀμηχάνους τὸ κάλλος. τὰ μὲν οὖν πολλά, ὦ Γλαύκων, πολλοῦ χρόνου διηγήσασθαι:

Chapter 4

τὸ δ' οὖν κεφάλαιον ἔφη τόδε εἶναι, ὅσα πώποτέ τινα ἠδίκησαν καὶ ὅσους ἕκαστοι, ὑπὲρ ἀπάντων δίκην δεδωκέναι ἐν μέρει, ὑπὲρ ἑκάστου δεκάκις-τοῦτο δ' εἶναι κατὰ ἑκατονταετηρίδα [615b] ἑκάστην, ὡς βίου ὄντος τοσούτου τοῦ ἀνθρωπίνου-ἵνα δεκαπλάσιον τὸ ἔκτεισμα τοῦ ἀδικήματος ἐκτίνοιεν, καὶ οἷον εἴ τινες πολλοῖς θανάτων ἦσαν αἴτιοι, ἤ

πόλεις προδόντες ἢ στρατόπεδα, καὶ εἰς δουλείας ἐμβεβληκότες ἤ τινος ἄλλης κακουχίας μεταίτιοι, πάντων τούτων
δεκαπλασίας ἀλγηδόνας ὑπὲρ ἑκάστου κομίσαιντο, καὶ αὖ
εἴ τινας εὐεργεσίας εὐεργετηκότες καὶ δίκαιοι καὶ ὅσιοι γεγονότες εἶεν, κατὰ ταὐτὰ [615c] τὴν ἀξίαν κομίζοιντο. τῶν
δὲ εὐθὺς γενομένων καὶ ὀλίγον χρόνον βιούντων πέρι ἄλλα
ἔλεγεν οὐκ ἄξια μνήμης. εἰς δὲ θεοὺς ἀσεβείας τε καὶ εὐσεβείας καὶ γονέας καὶ αὐτόχειρος φόνου μείζους ἔτι τοὺς μισθοὺς
διηγεῖτο.

Chapter 5

ἔφη γὰρ δὴ παραγενέσθαι ἐρωτωμένῳ ἑτέρῳ ὑπὸ ἑτέρου
ὅπου εἴη Ἀρδιαῖος ὁ μέγας. ὁ δὲ Ἀρδιαῖος οὗτος τῆς Παμφυλίας ἔν τινι πόλει τύραννος ἐγεγόνει, ἤδη χιλιοστὸν ἔτος εἰς
ἐκεῖνον τὸν χρόνον, γέροντά τε πατέρα ἀποκτείνας [615d]
καὶ πρεσβύτερον ἀδελφόν, καὶ ἄλλα δὴ πολλά τε καὶ ἀνόσια
εἰργασμένος, ὡς ἐλέγετο. ἔφη οὖν τὸν ἐρωτώμενον εἰπεῖν,
"οὐχ ἥκει," φάναι, "οὐδ᾽ ἂν ἥξει δεῦρο. ἐθεασάμεθα γὰρ οὖν
δὴ καὶ τοῦτο τῶν δεινῶν θεαμάτων· ἐπειδὴ ἐγγὺς τοῦ στομίου ἦμεν μέλλοντες ἀνιέναι καὶ τἆλλα πάντα πεπονθότες,
ἐκεῖνόν τε κατείδομεν ἐξαίφνης καὶ ἄλλους-σχεδόν τι αὐτῶν
τοὺς πλείστους τυράννους· ἦσαν δὲ καὶ ἰδιῶταί τινες τῶν
[615e] μεγάλα ἡμαρτηκότων-οὓς οἰομένους ἤδη ἀναβήσεσθαι οὐκ ἐδέχετο τὸ στόμιον, ἀλλ᾽ ἐμυκᾶτο ὁπότε τις τῶν
οὕτως ἀνιάτως ἐχόντων εἰς πονηρίαν ἢ μὴ ἱκανῶς δεδωκὼς
δίκην ἐπιχειροῖ ἀνιέναι. ἐνταῦθα δὴ ἄνδρες, ἔφη, ἄγριοι, διάπυροι ἰδεῖν, παρεστῶτες καὶ καταμανθάνοντες τὸ φθέγμα,
τοὺς μὲν διαλαβόντες ἦγον, τὸν δὲ Ἀρδιαῖον καὶ ἄλλους συμποδίσαντες [616a] χεῖράς τε καὶ πόδας καὶ κεφαλήν, καταβαλόντες καὶ ἐκδείραντες, εἷλκον παρὰ τὴν ὁδὸν ἐκτὸς ἐπ᾽

ἀσπαλάθων κνάμπτοντες, καὶ τοῖς ἀεὶ παριοῦσι σημαίνοντες ὧν ἕνεκά τε καὶ ὅτι εἰς τὸν Τάρταρον ἐμπεσούμενοι ἄγοιντο."

ἔνθα δὴ φόβων, ἔφη, πολλῶν καὶ παντοδαπῶν σφίσι γεγονότων, τοῦτον ὑπερβάλλειν, μὴ γένοιτο ἑκάστῳ τὸ φθέγμα ὅτε ἀναβαίνοι, καὶ ἀσμενέστατα ἕκαστον σιγήσαντος ἀναβῆναι. καὶ τὰς μὲν δὴ δίκας τε καὶ τιμωρίας τοιαύτας τινὰς [616b] εἶναι, καὶ αὖ τὰς εὐεργεσίας ταύταις ἀντιστρόφους.

Chapter 6

ἐπειδὴ δὲ τοῖς ἐν τῷ λειμῶνι ἑκάστοις ἑπτὰ ἡμέραι γένοιντο, ἀναστάντας ἐντεῦθεν δεῖν τῇ ὀγδόῃ πορεύεσθαι, καὶ ἀφικνεῖσθαι τεταρταίους ὅθεν καθορᾶν ἄνωθεν διὰ παντὸς τοῦ οὐρανοῦ καὶ γῆς τεταμένον φῶς εὐθύ, οἷον κίονα, μάλιστα τῇ ἴριδι προσφερῆ, λαμπρότερον δὲ καὶ καθαρώτερον· εἰς ὃ ἀφικέσθαι προελθόντες ἡμερησίαν ὁδόν, καὶ ἰδεῖν αὐτόθι κατὰ [616c] μέσον τὸ φῶς ἐκ τοῦ οὐρανοῦ τὰ ἄκρα αὐτοῦ τῶν δεσμῶν τεταμένα-εἶναι γὰρ τοῦτο τὸ φῶς σύνδεσμον τοῦ οὐρανοῦ, οἷον τὰ ὑποζώματα τῶν τριήρων, οὕτω πᾶσαν συνέχον τὴν περιφοράν-

Chapter 7

ἐκ δὲ τῶν ἄκρων τεταμένον ἀνάγκης ἄτρακτον, δι' οὗ πάσας ἐπιστρέφεσθαι τὰς περιφοράς· οὗ τὴν μὲν ἠλακάτην τε καὶ τὸ ἄγκιστρον εἶναι ἐξ ἀδάμαντος, τὸν δὲ σφόνδυλον μεικτὸν ἔκ τε τούτου καὶ ἄλλων γενῶν. τὴν δὲ [616d] τοῦ σφονδύλου φύσιν εἶναι τοιάνδε· τὸ μὲν σχῆμα οἷάπερ ἡ τοῦ ἐνθάδε, νοῆσαι δὲ δεῖ ἐξ ὧν ἔλεγεν τοιόνδε αὐτὸν εἶναι, ὥσπερ ἂν εἰ ἐν ἑνὶ μεγάλῳ σφονδύλῳ κοίλῳ καὶ ἐξεγλυμμένῳ διαμπερὲς ἄλλος τοιοῦτος ἐλάττων ἐγκέοιτο ἁρμόττων, καθάπερ οἱ κάδοι οἱ εἰς ἀλλήλους ἁρμόττοντες, καὶ οὕτω δὴ τρίτον ἄλλον καὶ τέταρτον καὶ ἄλλους τέτταρας. ὀκτὼ γὰρ εἶναι τοὺς σύμπαντας σφονδύλους, ἐν ἀλλήλοις ἐγκειμένους, [616e] κύκλους ἄνωθεν τὰ χείλη φαίνοντας, νῶτον συνεχὲς ἑνὸς σφονδύλου ἀπεργαζομένους περὶ τὴν ἠλακάτην· ἐκείνην δὲ διὰ μέσου τοῦ ὀγδόου διαμπερὲς ἐληλάσθαι.

Chapter 8

τὸν μὲν οὖν πρῶτόν τε καὶ ἐξωτάτω σφόνδυλον πλατύτατον τὸν τοῦ χείλους κύκλον ἔχειν, τὸν δὲ τοῦ ἕκτου δεύτερον, τρίτον δὲ τὸν τοῦ τετάρτου, τέταρτον δὲ τὸν τοῦ ὀγδόου, πέμπτον δὲ τὸν τοῦ ἑβδόμου, ἕκτον δὲ τὸν τοῦ πέμπτου, ἕβδομον δὲ τὸν τοῦ τρίτου, ὄγδοον δὲ τὸν τοῦ δευτέρου. καὶ τὸν μὲν τοῦ μεγίστου ποικίλον, τὸν δὲ τοῦ ἑβδόμου λαμπρότατον, τὸν δὲ [617a] τοῦ ὀγδόου τὸ χρῶμα ἀπὸ τοῦ ἑβδόμου ἔχειν προσλάμποντος, τὸν δὲ τοῦ δευτέρου καὶ πέμπτου παραπλήσια ἀλλήλοις, ξανθότερα ἐκείνων, τρίτον δὲ λευκότατον χρῶμα ἔχειν, τέταρτον δὲ ὑπέρυθρον, δεύτερον δὲ λευκότητι τὸν ἕκτον. κυκλεῖσθαι δὲ δὴ στρεφόμενον τὸν ἄτρακτον ὅλον μὲν τὴν αὐτὴν φοράν, ἐν δὲ τῷ ὅλῳ περιφερομένῳ τοὺς μὲν ἐντὸς ἑπτὰ κύκλους τὴν ἐναντίαν τῷ ὅλῳ ἠρέμα περιφέρεσθαι, αὐτῶν δὲ τούτων τάχιστα μὲν ἰέναι τὸν ὄγδοον, δευτέρους δὲ καὶ ἅμα [617b] ἀλλήλοις τόν τε ἕβδομον καὶ ἕκτον καὶ πέμπτον· [τὸν] τρίτον δὲ φορᾷ ἰέναι, ὡς σφίσι φαίνεσθαι, ἐπανακυκλούμενον τὸν τέταρτον, τέταρτον δὲ τὸν τρίτον καὶ πέμπτον τὸν δεύτερον. στρέφεσθαι δὲ αὐτὸν ἐν τοῖς τῆς ἀνάγκης γόνασιν. ἐπὶ δὲ τῶν κύκλων αὐτοῦ ἄνωθεν ἐφ' ἑκάστου βεβηκέναι Σειρῆνα συμπεριφερομένην, φωνὴν μίαν ἱεῖσαν, ἕνα τόνον· ἐκ πασῶν δὲ ὀκτὼ οὐσῶν μίαν ἁρμονίαν συμφωνεῖν.

13

Chapter 9

ἄλλας δὲ καθημένας [617c] πέριξ δι᾽ ἴσου τρεῖς, ἐν θρόνῳ ἑκάστην, θυγατέρας τῆς ἀνάγκης, Μοίρας, λευχειμονούσας, στέμματα ἐπὶ τῶν κεφαλῶν ἐχούσας, Λάχεσίν τε καὶ Κλωθὼ καὶ Ἄτροπον, ὑμνεῖν πρὸς τὴν τῶν Σειρήνων ἁρμονίαν, Λάχεσιν μὲν τὰ γεγονότα, Κλωθὼ δὲ τὰ ὄντα, Ἄτροπον δὲ τὰ μέλλοντα. καὶ τὴν μὲν Κλωθὼ τῇ δεξιᾷ χειρὶ ἐφαπτομένην συνεπιστρέφειν τοῦ ἀτράκτου τὴν ἔξω περιφοράν, διαλείπουσαν χρόνον, τὴν δὲ Ἄτροπον τῇ ἀριστερᾷ τὰς ἐντὸς αὖ ὡσαύτως· τὴν δὲ Λάχεσιν [617d] ἐν μέρει ἑκατέρας ἑκατέρᾳ τῇ χειρὶ ἐφάπτεσθαι. σφᾶς οὖν, ἐπειδὴ ἀφικέσθαι, εὐθὺς δεῖν ἰέναι πρὸς τὴν Λάχεσιν. προφήτην οὖν τινα σφᾶς πρῶτον μὲν ἐν τάξει διαστῆσαι, ἔπειτα λαβόντα ἐκ τῶν τῆς Λαχέσεως γονάτων κλήρους τε καὶ βίων παραδείγματα, ἀναβάντα ἐπί τι βῆμα ὑψηλὸν εἰπεῖν-

Chapter 10

«ἀνάγκης θυγατρὸς κόρης Λαχέσεως λόγος. Ψυχαὶ ἐφήμεροι, ἀρχὴ ἄλλης περιόδου θνητοῦ γένους θανατηφόρου. [617e] οὐχ ὑμᾶς δαίμων λήξεται, ἀλλ᾽ ὑμεῖς δαίμονα αἱρήσεσθε. πρῶτος δ᾽ ὁ λαχὼν πρῶτος αἱρείσθω βίον ᾧ συνέσται ἐξ ἀνάγκης. ἀρετὴ δὲ ἀδέσποτον, ἣν τιμῶν καὶ ἀτιμάζων πλέον καὶ ἔλαττον αὐτῆς ἕκαστος ἕξει. αἰτία ἑλομένου· θεὸς ἀναίτιος.»

Chapter 11

ταῦτα εἰπόντα ῥῖψαι ἐπὶ πάντας τοὺς κλήρους, τὸν δὲ παρ᾽ αὐτὸν πεσόντα ἕκαστον ἀναιρεῖσθαι πλὴν οὗ, ἃ δὲ οὐκ ἐᾶν· τῷ δὲ ἀνελομένῳ δῆλον εἶναι ὁπόστος εἴληχει. [618a] μετὰ δὲ τοῦτο αὖθις τὰ τῶν βίων παραδείγματα εἰς τὸ πρόσθεν σφῶν θεῖναι ἐπὶ τὴν γῆν, πολὺ πλείω τῶν παρόντων. εἶναι δὲ παντοδαπά: ζῴων τε γὰρ πάντων βίους καὶ δὴ καὶ τοὺς ἀνθρωπίνους ἅπαντας. τυραννίδας τε γὰρ ἐν αὐτοῖς εἶναι, τὰς μὲν διατελεῖς, τὰς δὲ καὶ μεταξὺ διαφθειρομένας καὶ εἰς πενίας τε καὶ φυγὰς καὶ εἰς πτωχείας τελευτώσας: εἶναι δὲ καὶ δοκίμων ἀνδρῶν βίους, τοὺς μὲν ἐπὶ εἴδεσιν καὶ κατὰ κάλλη καὶ τὴν ἄλλην ἰσχύν [618b] τε καὶ ἀγωνίαν, τοὺς δ' ἐπὶ γένεσιν καὶ προγόνων ἀρεταῖς, καὶ ἀδοκίμων κατὰ ταῦτα, ὡσαύτως δὲ καὶ γυναικῶν. ψυχῆς δὲ τάξιν οὐκ ἐνεῖναι διὰ τὸ ἀναγκαίως ἔχειν ἄλλον ἑλομένην βίον ἀλλοίαν γίγνεσθαι: τὰ δ' ἄλλα ἀλλήλοις τε καὶ πλούτοις καὶ πενίαις, τὰ δὲ νόσοις, τὰ δ' ὑγιείαις μεμεῖχθαι, τὰ δὲ καὶ μεσοῦν τούτων.

Chapter 12

ἔνθα δή, ὡς ἔοικεν, ὦ φίλε Γλαύκων, ὁ πᾶς κίνδυνος ἀνθρώπῳ, καὶ διὰ ταῦτα μάλιστα [618c] ἐπιμελητέον ὅπως ἕκαστος ἡμῶν τῶν ἄλλων μαθημάτων ἀμελήσας τούτου τοῦ μαθήματος καὶ ζητητὴς καὶ μαθητὴς ἔσται, ἐάν ποθεν οἷός τ' ᾖ μαθεῖν καὶ ἐξευρεῖν τίς αὐτὸν ποιήσει δυνατὸν καὶ ἐπιστήμονα, βίον καὶ χρηστὸν καὶ πονηρὸν διαγιγνώσκοντα, τὸν βελτίω ἐκ τῶν δυνατῶν ἀεὶ πανταχοῦ αἱρεῖσθαι: ἀναλογιζόμενον πάντα τὰ νυνδὴ ῥηθέντα καὶ συντιθέμενα ἀλλήλοις καὶ διαιρούμενα πρὸς ἀρετὴν βίου πῶς ἔχει, εἰδέναι τί κάλλος πενίᾳ ἢ πλούτῳ κραθὲν καὶ [618d] μετὰ ποίας τινὸς ψυχῆς ἕξεως κακὸν ἢ ἀγαθὸν ἐργάζεται, καὶ τί εὐγένειαι καὶ δυσγένειαι καὶ ἰδιωτεῖαι καὶ ἀρχαὶ καὶ ἰσχύες καὶ ἀσθένειαι καὶ εὐμαθίαι καὶ δυσμαθίαι καὶ πάντα τὰ τοιαῦτα τῶν φύσει περὶ ψυχὴν ὄντων καὶ τῶν ἐπικτήτων τί συγκεραννύμενα πρὸς ἄλληλα ἐργάζεται, ὥστε ἐξ ἁπάντων αὐτῶν δυνατὸν εἶναι συλλογισάμενον αἱρεῖσθαι, πρὸς τὴν τῆς ψυχῆς φύσιν ἀποβλέποντα, τόν τε χείρω καὶ τὸν ἀμείνω [618e] βίον, χείρω μὲν καλοῦντα ὃς αὐτὴν ἐκεῖσε ἄξει, εἰς τὸ ἀδικωτέραν γίγνεσθαι, ἀμείνω δὲ ὅστις εἰς τὸ δικαιοτέραν.

Chapter 13

τὰ δὲ ἄλλα πάντα χαίρειν ἐάσει· ἑωράκαμεν γὰρ ὅτι ζῶντί τε καὶ τελευτήσαντι αὕτη κρατίστη αἵρεσις. ἀδαμαντίνως δὴ [619a] δεῖ ταύτην τὴν δόξαν ἔχοντα εἰς Ἅιδου ἰέναι, ὅπως ἂν ᾖ καὶ ἐκεῖ ἀνέκπληκτος ὑπὸ πλούτων τε καὶ τῶν τοιούτων κακῶν, καὶ μὴ ἐμπεσὼν εἰς τυραννίδας καὶ ἄλλας τοιαύτας πράξεις πολλὰ μὲν ἐργάσηται καὶ ἀνήκεστα κακά, ἔτι δὲ αὐτὸς μείζω πάθῃ, ἀλλὰ γνῷ τὸν μέσον ἀεὶ τῶν τοιούτων βίον αἱρεῖσθαι καὶ φεύγειν τὰ ὑπερβάλλοντα ἑκατέρωσε καὶ ἐν τῷδε τῷ βίῳ κατὰ τὸ δυνατὸν καὶ ἐν παντὶ τῷ ἔπειτα· οὕτω γὰρ [619b] εὐδαιμονέστατος γίγνεται ἄνθρωπος. καὶ δὴ οὖν καὶ τότε ὁ ἐκεῖθεν ἄγγελος ἤγγελλε τὸν μὲν προφήτην οὕτως εἰπεῖν· «καὶ τελευταίῳ ἐπιόντι, ξὺν νῷ ἑλομένῳ, συντόνως ζῶντι κεῖται βίος ἀγαπητός, οὐ κακός. μήτε ὁ ἄρχων αἱρέσεως ἀμελείτω μήτε ὁ τελευτῶν ἀθυμείτω.»

Chapter 14

εἰπόντος δὲ ταῦτα τὸν πρῶτον λαχόντα ἔφη εὐθὺς ἐπιόντα τὴν μεγίστην τυραννίδα ἑλέσθαι, καὶ ὑπὸ ἀφροσύνης τε καὶ λαιμαργίας οὐ πάντα ἱκανῶς ἀνασκεψάμενον ἑλέσθαι, ἀλλ᾽ [619c] αὐτὸν λαθεῖν ἐνοῦσαν εἱμαρμένην παίδων αὐτοῦ βρώσεις καὶ ἄλλα κακά· ἐπειδὴ δὲ κατὰ σχολὴν σκέψασθαι, κόπτεσθαί τε καὶ ὀδύρεσθαι τὴν αἵρεσιν, οὐκ ἐμμένοντα τοῖς προρρηθεῖσιν ὑπὸ τοῦ προφήτου· οὐ γὰρ ἑαυτὸν αἰτιᾶσθαι τῶν κακῶν, ἀλλὰ τύχην τε καὶ δαίμονας καὶ πάντα μᾶλλον ἀνθ᾽ ἑαυτοῦ. εἶναι δὲ αὐτὸν τῶν ἐκ τοῦ οὐρανοῦ ἡκόντων, ἐν τεταγμένῃ πολιτείᾳ ἐν τῷ προτέρῳ βίῳ βεβιωκότα, ἔθει

[619d] ἄνευ φιλοσοφίας ἀρετῆς μετειληφότα. ὡς δὲ καὶ εἰπεῖν, οὐκ ἐλάττους εἶναι ἐν τοῖς τοιούτοις ἁλισκομένους τοὺς ἐκ τοῦ οὐρανοῦ ἥκοντας, ἅτε πόνων ἀγυμνάστους· τῶν δ᾽ ἐκ τῆς γῆς τοὺς πολλούς, ἅτε αὐτούς τε πεπονηκότας ἄλλους τε ἑωρακότας, οὐκ ἐξ ἐπιδρομῆς τὰς αἱρέσεις ποιεῖσθαι. διὸ δὴ καὶ μεταβολὴν τῶν κακῶν καὶ τῶν ἀγαθῶν ταῖς πολλαῖς τῶν ψυχῶν γίγνεσθαι καὶ διὰ τὴν τοῦ κλήρου τύχην· ἐπεὶ εἴ τις ἀεί, ὁπότε εἰς τὸν ἐνθάδε βίον ἀφικνοῖτο, ὑγιῶς φιλοσοφοῖ [619e] καὶ ὁ κλῆρος αὐτῷ τῆς αἱρέσεως μὴ ἐν τελευταίοις πίπτοι, κινδυνεύει ἐκ τῶν ἐκεῖθεν ἀπαγγελλομένων οὐ μόνον ἐνθάδε εὐδαιμονεῖν ἄν, ἀλλὰ καὶ τὴν ἐνθένδε ἐκεῖσε καὶ δεῦρο πάλιν πορείαν οὐκ ἂν χθονίαν καὶ τραχεῖαν πορεύεσθαι, ἀλλὰ λείαν τε καὶ οὐρανίαν.

Chapter 15

ταύτην γὰρ δὴ ἔφη τὴν θέαν ἀξίαν εἶναι ἰδεῖν, ὡς ἕκασται [620a] αἱ ψυχαὶ ᾑροῦντο τοὺς βίους· ἐλεινήν τε γὰρ ἰδεῖν εἶναι καὶ γελοίαν καὶ θαυμασίαν. κατὰ συνήθειαν γὰρ τοῦ προτέρου βίου τὰ πολλὰ αἱρεῖσθαι. ἰδεῖν μὲν γὰρ ψυχὴν ἔφη τήν ποτε Ὀρφέως γενομένην κύκνου βίον αἱρουμένην, μίσει τοῦ γυναικείου γένους διὰ τὸν ὑπ᾽ ἐκείνων θάνατον οὐκ ἐθέλουσαν ἐν γυναικὶ γεννηθεῖσαν γενέσθαι· ἰδεῖν δὲ τὴν Θαμύρου ἀηδόνος ἑλομένην· ἰδεῖν δὲ καὶ κύκνον μεταβάλλοντα εἰς ἀνθρωπίνου βίου αἵρεσιν, καὶ ἄλλα ζῷα μουσικὰ ὡσαύτως. [620b] εἰκοστὴν δὲ λαχοῦσαν ψυχὴν ἑλέσθαι λέοντος βίον· εἶναι δὲ τὴν Αἴαντος τοῦ Τελαμωνίου, φεύγουσαν ἄνθρωπον γενέσθαι, μεμνημένην τῆς τῶν ὅπλων κρίσεως. τὴν δ᾽ ἐπὶ τούτῳ Ἀγαμέμνονος· ἔχθρᾳ δὲ καὶ ταύτην τοῦ ἀνθρωπίνου γένους διὰ τὰ πάθη ἀετοῦ διαλλάξαι βίον. ἐν μέσοις δὲ λαχοῦσαν τὴν Ἀταλάντης ψυχήν, κατιδοῦσαν μεγάλας τιμὰς

17

ἀθλητοῦ ἀνδρός, οὐ δύνασθαι παρελθεῖν, ἀλλὰ λαβεῖν. μετὰ [620c] δὲ ταύτην ἰδεῖν τὴν Ἐπειοῦ τοῦ Πανοπέως εἰς τεχνικῆς γυναικὸς ἰοῦσαν φύσιν· πόρρω δ' ἐν ὑστάτοις ἰδεῖν τὴν τοῦ γελωτοποιοῦ Θερσίτου πίθηκον ἐνδυομένην. κατὰ τύχην δὲ τὴν Ὀδυσσέως λαχοῦσαν πασῶν ὑστάτην αἱρησομένην ἰέναι, μνήμῃ δὲ τῶν προτέρων πόνων φιλοτιμίας λελωφηκυῖαν ζητεῖν περιοῦσαν χρόνον πολὺν βίον ἀνδρὸς ἰδιώτου ἀπράγμονος, καὶ μόγις εὑρεῖν κείμενόν που καὶ παρημελημένον [620d] ὑπὸ τῶν ἄλλων, καὶ εἰπεῖν ἰδοῦσαν ὅτι τὰ αὐτὰ ἂν ἔπραξεν καὶ πρώτη λαχοῦσα, καὶ ἁσμένην ἑλέσθαι. καὶ ἐκ τῶν ἄλλων δὴ θηρίων ὡσαύτως εἰς ἀνθρώπους ἰέναι καὶ εἰς ἄλληλα, τὰ μὲν ἄδικα εἰς τὰ ἄγρια, τὰ δὲ δίκαια εἰς τὰ ἥμερα μεταβάλλοντα, καὶ πάσας μείξεις μείγνυσθαι.

Chapter 16

ἐπειδὴ δ' οὖν πάσας τὰς ψυχὰς τοὺς βίους ᾑρῆσθαι, ὥσπερ ἔλαχον ἐν τάξει προσιέναι πρὸς τὴν Λάχεσιν· ἐκείνην δ' ἐκάστῳ ὃν εἵλετο δαίμονα, τοῦτον φύλακα συμπέμπειν [620e] τοῦ βίου καὶ ἀποπληρωτὴν τῶν αἱρεθέντων. ὃν πρῶτον μὲν ἄγειν αὐτὴν πρὸς τὴν Κλωθὼ ὑπὸ τὴν ἐκείνης χεῖρά τε καὶ ἐπιστροφὴν τῆς τοῦ ἀτράκτου δίνης, κυροῦντα ἣν λαχὼν εἵλετο μοῖραν· ταύτης δ' ἐφαψάμενον αὖθις ἐπὶ τὴν τῆς Ἀτρόπου ἄγειν νῆσιν, ἀμετάστροφα τὰ ἐπικλωσθέντα ποιοῦντα· ἐντεῦθεν δὲ δὴ ἀμεταστρεπτὶ ὑπὸ τὸν τῆς [621a] ἀνάγκης ἰέναι θρόνον, καὶ δι' ἐκείνου διεξελθόντα, ἐπειδὴ καὶ οἱ ἄλλοι διῆλθον, πορεύεσθαι ἅπαντας εἰς τὸ τῆς Λήθης πεδίον διὰ καύματός τε καὶ πνίγους δεινοῦ· καὶ γὰρ εἶναι αὐτὸ κενὸν δένδρων τε καὶ ὅσα γῆ φύει. σκηνᾶσθαι οὖν σφᾶς ἤδη ἑσπέρας γιγνομένης παρὰ τὸν Ἀμέλητα ποταμόν, οὗ τὸ ὕδωρ ἀγγεῖον οὐδὲν στέγειν. μέτρον μὲν οὖν τι τοῦ ὕδατος πᾶσιν

ἀναγκαῖον εἶναι πιεῖν, τοὺς δὲ φρονήσει μὴ σῳζομένους
πλέον πίνειν τοῦ μέτρου· τὸν δὲ ἀεὶ πιόντα [621b] πάντων
ἐπιλανθάνεσθαι. ἐπειδὴ δὲ κοιμηθῆναι καὶ μέσας νύκτας γενέσθαι, βροντήν τε καὶ σεισμὸν γενέσθαι, καὶ ἐντεῦθεν ἐξαπίνης ἄλλον ἄλλῃ φέρεσθαι ἄνω εἰς τὴν γένεσιν, ᾄττοντας
ὥσπερ ἀστέρας. αὐτὸς δὲ τοῦ μὲν ὕδατος κωλυθῆναι πιεῖν·
ὅπῃ μέντοι καὶ ὅπως εἰς τὸ σῶμα ἀφίκοιτο, οὐκ εἰδέναι, ἀλλ'
ἐξαίφνης ἀναβλέψας ἰδεῖν ἕωθεν αὐτὸν κείμενον ἐπὶ τῇ πυρᾷ.

Chapter 17

καὶ οὕτως, ὦ Γλαύκων, μῦθος ἐσώθη καὶ οὐκ ἀπώλετο,
[621c] καὶ ἡμᾶς ἂν σώσειεν, ἂν πειθώμεθα αὐτῷ, καὶ τὸν τῆς
Λήθης ποταμὸν εὖ διαβησόμεθα καὶ τὴν ψυχὴν οὐ μιανθησόμεθα. ἀλλ' ἂν ἐμοὶ πειθώμεθα, νομίζοντες ἀθάνατον ψυχὴν
καὶ δυνατὴν πάντα μὲν κακὰ ἀνέχεσθαι, πάντα δὲ ἀγαθά,
τῆς ἄνω ὁδοῦ ἀεὶ ἑξόμεθα καὶ δικαιοσύνην μετὰ φρονήσεως
παντὶ τρόπῳ ἐπιτηδεύσομεν, ἵνα καὶ ἡμῖν αὐτοῖς φίλοι ὦμεν
καὶ τοῖς θεοῖς, αὐτοῦ τε μένοντες ἐνθάδε, καὶ ἐπειδὰν τὰ ἆθλα
[621d] αὐτῆς κομιζώμεθα, ὥσπερ οἱ νικηφόροι περιαγειρόμενοι, καὶ ἐνθάδε καὶ ἐν τῇ χιλιέτει πορείᾳ, ἣν διεληλύθαμεν,
εὖ πράττωμεν.

Preface

From the first moment we come into contact with a purely philosophical text, we must be open to the possibility that it was written in order to reveal to us unknown and unexplored aspects of our souls, and to assist us in discovering and decoding the hidden truth, which is very difficult to understand. This is an issue upon which we ought to direct our attention and study.

A truly necessary prerequisite for such a study is to have realized in advance that the philosophical texts require a totally different approach and we should never treat them in the way we unfortunately follow many times, that is as if they were just pieces of literature.

One indisputable fact should not escape from our attention: that an ancient Greek philosophical text hides inside it a whole spiritual world, totally different from our everyday thoughts. We should feel a real need to penetrate into this unknown new world, and to employ all our capacities in order to understand its content.

We should also be willing to allocate ample time and to enlist all of our knowledge in order to be able to make contact with these hidden truths; the first step towards this end is to determine up to which point we can follow the thought of the ancient writer, Plato in the case of this book.

Having detected our lack of knowledge, I think it is necessary to turn our attention to the sciences related to the content of the ancient text, and then to study the corresponding scientific theories that we do not know, even if they are specialized, since otherwise it may be impossible to proceed to the correct interpretation of certain passages.

I believe that the primary aim of an ancient text, even before we tackle its philosophical dimension, is to force us to realize the need to upgrade our knowledge, perhaps to study sciences we had never studied before, and to broaden our intellectual awareness. Besides, we must not forget that almost all ancient Greek philosophical writers had a grasp of all the scientific knowledge that was available at their period.

Only after an integrated and complete research, and an even greater preparation in order to accept and understand the true meaning will we be allowed to decipher it and to gradually approach the wisdom of the ancient text.

Armed by our thorough preparation, we realize from the beginning that all the elements and information we are about to study in depth can have more than one interpretations and they are never just an elegant fairy tale, although its title can be, as in the case of this book, "the myth of Er".

We now know that, in the texts of all ancient civilisations, the metaphysical content is always expressed in terms of myths, oracles, riddles, parables, or even, as in this particular case, with a wordplay. It is a particular way of communication, which is used only when mystery-related serious topics are concerned, thus resisting their revelation. A revelation that, in order to be able to understand it, it is necessary to exceed our powers and conventional interpretations, if we are to benefit from it.

In the age of ancient Greece the encoding of the great philosophical notions that refer to life and death was absolutely necessary, since they were considered higher knowledge for the initiated ones. This knowledge was forbidden to be publicized, because there was the danger to be both misunderstood and misinterpreted, with catastrophic consequences for the ignorant person.

Of course, this interdiction is no longer valid, since there are no more mystic institutions associated with philosophical schools to impose it. Unfortunately, however, we live in an age that has generated a similar result of misinterpretation, caused mainly by the brutal treatment of the ancient Greek texts. It is a fact that in the conventional translations that were attempted not the slightest effort was ever made to interpret this internal dimension that is hidden inside them, thus depriving us from the valuable and often redeeming philosophical knowledge.

As a rule, when we come into contact with a philosophical text we commonly neglect totally the higher-order philosophical meanings that are hidden behind its lines. The published translations are restricted to a typical transfer of the words in their correct syntax of "subject-verb-object", or they follow a verbatim style and the readers should not be impressed if the result often distorts the content of the ancient text, or if at best it is meaningless.

Hence we should make clear, before we launch this new effort to interpret and analyze the ancient Platonic text, that we do not aim at a superficial and trivial interpretation, devoid of any possibility to reveal the true reason for its creation. On the contrary, our intention is to enter from the start this "wordplay" Plato invites us to participate in, and to attempt to discover other meanings, even unconventional ones. To attempt to understand the advanced scientific knowledge that is probably hidden under the disguise of the myth and, through his own witty wordplay, to participate in and, if we can, to conquer this singular education, which could subsequently transform our lives.

This is exactly what should be the expected result of our occupation with the Platonic text. Of course, in such a case we should accept as a necessary hypothesis that these philosophical "sacred" texts are written in a way that offers us at least two distinct levels of interpretation:

- The level of the superficial approach, which corresponds to every reader who will read the text because it just happened to fall in their hands. It is not expected for such a casual reader to be able to discover and to understand the deeper truth, for the simple reason that he or she is not interested in this higher knowledge, let alone that he could not easily understand it.

- The level of a purely esoteric philosophical in-depth approach, of a "second reading", which is directed towards those readers who already possess some necessary knowledge and who are truly interested in understanding the hidden secrets, because they know that this way they can proceed to higher levels of knowledge.

The approach followed in this book belongs, of course, to the second level: to those readers who consciously want to approach a wider or higher truth and who are impressed by the wealth of knowledge and of revelations, which no one could easily imagine that they could possibly be contained in an ancient text.

In order to realize the meticulously hidden potentiality of this ancient "sacred" text and the higher knowledge that it probably contains, it is absolutely necessary to approach it in a completely different way than the way in which we are used to read the ancient texts up to now.

Also, in order to better understand the hidden meanings and to reach certain safe conclusions, we should have a concise knowledge of as many texts of Platonic philosophy as possible.

Plato himself had explained in his dialogue *Cratylus* the method by which we can analyze and understand the hidden meaning behind every "sacred" word, which, according to his view, has been constructed in purpose, in order to encrypt the true higher notion (philosophical or scientific).

In this particular case, however, we face something much more than a text that just contains encoded words and secret meanings. We face a "myth", that is a text we know from the start that its content needs a metaphorical interpretation, as the author himself warns us.

This means that, if one wants to approach this text correctly, one should necessarily want to understand the hidden meaning, something requiring that one is at a corresponding state of open mind and of positive inclination, which will allow to understand and process novel and different knowledge.

We also have to mention beforehand an important "detail" that lies not far from the end of the text, where Plato himself, using the mouth of Socrates, announces clearly that whatever has been said in the context of this myth is absolutely true in its entirety; and, moreover, that it is necessary to be understood and accepted from those readers who want to enter this spiritual path of the salvation of their souls, and to acquire this "forbidden" knowledge.

INTERPRETATION
OF THE ANCIENT TEXT

Chapter 1
THE SECRET IDENTITY OF ER

Ἀλλ' οὐ μέντοι σοι, ἦν δ' ἐγώ, Ἀλκίνου γε ἀπόλογον ἐρῶ, ἀλλ' ἀλκίμου μὲν ἀνδρός, Ἡρὸς τοῦ Ἀρμενίου, τὸ γένος Παμφύλου· ὅς ποτε ἐν πολέμῳ τελευτήσας, ἀναιρεθέντων δεκαταίων τῶν νεκρῶν ἤδη διεφθαρμένων, ὑγιὴς μὲν ἀνῃρέθη, κομισθεὶς δ' οἴκαδε μέλλων θάπτεσθαι δωδεκαταῖος ἐπὶ τῇ πυρᾷ κείμενος ἀνεβίω, ἀναβιοὺς δ' ἔλεγεν ἃ ἐκεῖ ἴδοι.

Ἀλλ' οὐ μέντοι σοι, ἦν δ' ἐγώ, Ἀλκίνου γε ἀπόλογον ἐρῶ, ἀλλ' ἀλκίμου μὲν ἀνδρός...

... After all this, Socrates said, I would like to relate the life of a person who doesn't have the characteristics of Alcinous, but those of a bold man;...

... Ἡρὸς τοῦ Ἀρμενίου, τὸ γένος Παμφύλου...

... this is the case of Er, an Armenian who was a descendant of Pamphylus.

We notice that Plato chooses to open the mystic tale or "myth of Er" by using a wordplay or pun: he juxtaposes the Greek words *Alkinou* = "of Alcinous" and *Alkimou* = "of a bold and powerful"; two words that sound almost the same, since they differ by only one letter.

...ὅς ποτε ἐν πολέμῳ τελευτήσας, ...

This man, after he was killed in a war,...

... ἀναιρεθέντων δεκαταίων τῶν νεκρῶν ἤδη διεφθαρμένων, ...

and after the corpses were taken up on the tenth day already decayed,...

... ὑγιὴς μὲν ἀνῃρέθη, ...

he (his body) was found and taken up intact.

... κομισθεὶς δ᾽ οἴκαδε μέλλων θάπτεσθαι δωδεκαταῖος ἐπὶ τῇ πυρᾷ κείμενος ἀνεβίω, ...

And when, on the twelfth day, his body was carried to his homeland for his funeral, as it lay upon the pyre to be cremated, it revived!

So the myth of Er has to do with the recording of an exceptionally important and rare event, which is directly connected to metaphysics!

It describes the travel taken by the soul of a man who,

while he was apparently dead, his body was preserved totally uncorrupted for 12 whole days, after which he became alive again, returning to the normal state he was before his death.

To begin, then, our analysis of the ancient text, we must understand that the narration that will follow describes a situation nowadays known as an out-of-body experience (OBE), the mechanism of which is totally unknown.

This is the point where the great interest of this text lies, because the story Plato is about to narrate in every detail concerns the wandering of the soul of Er in an invisible world, during the twelve days it had been separated from its body.

Hence, we realize that this is definitely a mystical and occult text, which will reveal to us the function of the invisible world. However, in order to be able to understand and of course to make use of this function to the extent this is possible to us, we should acquire the necessary knowledge.

... ἀναβιοὺς δ' ἔλεγεν ἃ ἐκεῖ ἴδοι.

And after coming to life he started to relate what one would imagine he had experienced where he was as a dead person.

The word *ekei* ("where he was") can be held to refer to the underworld, the realm of Hades. It should be thus realized that the meaning of the description that will follow is unique in Plato's dialogues and, of course, invaluable.

Each reader is about to become a witness of this totally unknown mystical procedure of the wandering of our souls in their after-death state; a procedure that will be described in its entirety and will offer to us the possibility to better understand the way in which we should handle our life for as long as we are "incarnated" according to the beliefs Plato apparently adopts in the "Myth of Er".

There is probably no other text in the whole Greek literature so clearly and illuminatingly supportive of the existence and metaphysical "function" of this invisible world, which in Plato is connected with the World of Ideas. This is perhaps the reason the author chooses to present it under the safe veil of a "myth".

Therefore, there is the need to employ all our forces in order to penetrate into the deepest layers of Platonic philosophy and to understand his views on the way the human soul exists after death.

Let us start from the fact that the ancient text begins with a wordplay. Two words that differ by only one letter are used: the name of ALKINOU is juxtaposed to the property of ALKIMOU. Let us try to enter the logic of this pun and to analyze the hidden meanings it contains.

Alcinous (*Alkinous*) is the well-known hero of Homer, the king of the Phaiacians; as the etymology of his Greek name implies, he is presumably the one who possesses a powerful and evolved mind, as an analogy with a strong body (*alke* = corporal strength, also the strength of the soul, bravery, courage; *nous* = mind). Similarly, *Alkimos* corresponds to the main characteristic of Er, the bold, powerful, healthy and evolved body, will and soul.

Hence, what is declared to us right from the start is that in the following story we will not have to do with persons that possess an evolved mind, but rather with persons that possess an evolved soul and will, for obviously this case is of considerably more interest.

We should know that the topic of the conquest of arete (virtue) is a celebrated occupation of philosophers. Arete, however, is an extremely complex and multifaceted notion, which would require a whole treatise by itself (and many such treatises have been written...) to be analyzed. Here it is sufficient to remind that Aristotle in his work *Nicomachean Ethics* sets two fundamental categories of virtues:

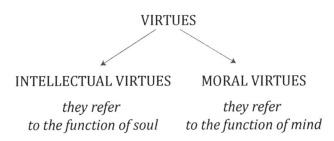

VIRTUES

INTELLECTUAL VIRTUES   MORAL VIRTUES

they refer   *they refer*
to the function of soul   *to the function of mind*

The intellectual virtues concern the proper function of the mind of a person while on the other hand the moral virtues have to do with the proper function of his or her soul.

So in the particular case presented by Plato, Alci*nous* is the person who employs only the virtues of *nous*, the intellectual virtues, while on the other side the *alkimos* Er is the person who appears as an integrated entity-personality, because in addition he employs also the moral virtues.

After these elucidations, we can better comprehend this wordplay of Plato. We know that Alcinous the king was the son of Nausithous and son or grandson of Periboea. From his father's side, Alcinous was grandson of Poseidon, the god of sea, while from his mother's side he was the great grandchild of Eurymedon, the king of the Giants.

Homer tells us that the people of Alcinous, the Phaiacians, were well-known for their capabilities as a seafaring nation (*nausiklytoi*) and for this reason they were the beloved people of Poseidon, being called "relatives of god". Initially, they lived in the remote region of Hypereia, near the edge of the world. When their king was Nausithous, the father of Alcinous, they were forced to migrate by the Cyclopes to the island of Scheria, which was renamed "the Island of the Phaiacians" or Phaeacia. The most impressive piece of information about the Phaiacians mentioned by Homer is about their remarkable ships, which were endowed by Poseidon with almost miraculous capabilities: Unlike the common ships of that age, they had no rudders, nor oars, and they could traverse the sea as if they had wings, while they could understand the human thoughts (*Odyssey*, Book VIII, 555-563).

By correlating these elements from Greek mythology with what the Greek language can reveal, we could extend Plato's pun to Homer: the genitive case PHAIAKON (= of the Phaiacians) could be imaginatively taken as a composite, from the words "phaia" and "akon". The first word, *phaia*, readily connects us to the term *phaia ousia*, the grey matter of the brain, which contains most of the brain's cell bodies, pointing to the strong mental abilities of the Phaiacians.

However, the second word, *akon*, which means lack of will (lit. "without his will", unwillingly), reveals that these strong mental abilities are not necessarily followed by a strong decision-making ability. Because mental abilities have to do mostly with the capacity to discover new things or to invent advanced new technology, or at a lower level to perform tasks that nowadays are done by computers; while in order to make important decisions one has often to employ his or her free will, an exclusively human function.

Summarizing the above in the context of the Platonic text, we could conclude that Alcinous and the strong mind have to do with the function of the brain, while the *alkimos* Er and free will have to do with the function of a healthy and evolved soul.

In other words, according to the Homeric description, the Phaiacians possessed the equivalent of an advanced technology, as we would say nowadays. However, it seems that this technology did not offer to them the powers necessary to avoid their fleeing from their country, Hypereia. The word *hypereia* in turn denotes a state of *hyper-roe*, a "superior flux" or flowing of soul energy required by the free will in order to function in a proper way, something that did not work in the case of the Phaiacians, while it presumably worked in the case of the soul energy flux of the alkimos Er, which we will examine. Once again, the forms of the genitive cases ROES (of the flux) and EROS (of Er) play a pun, being an anagram of one another.

In our interpretation of the myth, the Phaiacians manifested two functions with very different quality levels: From the one side there was an advanced mental capability, while from the other side there were real difficulties in the function of the soul. However, it seems that under these conditions the state of a human or of a group of humans cannot evolve.

A parallel with the case of Phaiacians can be found in the case of the Atlanteans, the dwellers of the legendary Atlantis who, according to Plato had also to flee from their homeland, because of the destruction of Atlantis brought about by themselves.

Unfortunately, as one can understand, similar tendencies characterize more and more our contemporary civilisation, which have not yet been adequately realized. It could be suggested that the reason Plato relates this myth, as an example of the evolution of the soul, at the end of his *Republic*, is that he wants to draw the attention of the future reader to the way his or her society lives; the globalized Western society of the 21st century of course operates in a way he would consider as an example of what to avoid.

In other words, Plato, as a great psychologist, knows that humans can achieve real evolution only when their mental progress, and in extension the advancement of technology that follows it, is accompanied necessarily by a corresponding evolution of their souls. Otherwise, we are heading towards a future disaster, such as the flight of the Phaiacians or of the Atlanteans as refugees. Plato is the only author who refers in two of his works, *Timaeus* and *Critias*, to the war between the Atlanteans and the Athenians, and to the eventual destruction of Atlantis. The crucial thing here is to understand the reason why the Athenians were able to win the Atlanteans, while the Phaiacians lost to the Cyclopes.

And the reason was that the PHAIA *ousia*, the "grey matter", of the Athenians was not AKON, as in the case of the PHAIAKON, but EKON, which means that it was accompanied by a well-developed free will, thanks to a gift by goddess Athena, who had offered them a virtue of the soul, *sophrosyne* (prudence, judiciousness).

We should contrast the meaning of the words *akon* (= without his will, unwillingly) and *ekon* (= with his will, willingly). When the grey matter of our brain is *akon*, this means that our mind operates based only on the intellectual virtue of wisdom in the sense of knowledgeability, which, as experience has shown, is not enough. When, on the other hand, our grey matter is *ekon*, then our mind operates according to the soul virtue of sophrosyne. Athena is a personification of and offers both virtues: the intellectual virtue of wisdom and the moral virtue of sophrosyne. This is the reason the Athenians won the Atlanteans; the latter possessed only wisdom and technological superiority, while the former possessed in addition the moral virtue of prudence.

Why, then Plato announces that he will not tell the story of Alcinous, but that of another, *alkimos* man, who in this case is Er, a soldier?

Presumably, because the case of Alcinous would be a negative example, as accompanied only by wisdom, while on the contrary the case of Er should be a positive example, since it combines wisdom and prudence in an ideal state of human behaviour. The word *alkimos* means bold, strong, powerful, invincible, resisting, durable. We should understand that in the text these properties refer at a first level to the body, while at a higher level they refer to the main characteristics of the soul acquired through prudence and the proper function of free will, and not through wisdom.

Alcinous represents an unbalanced state between the functions of the mind and those of the soul, while the *alkimos* Er represents a balanced state, which was achieved thanks to the evolution of his soul, an evolution cultivated during his life.

Under this unusual and peculiar name, Er, is probably hidden the word hERa. As a person's name, Hera refers to the Olympian goddess, the wife of Zeus and the goddess-protector of marriage and married women, who also symbolizes the notion of the universal soul, including the collective soul of the mankind: If, according to our decoding of Greek mythology, Zeus is a symbol for the mind, then, correspondingly, his wife, Hera, stands as a symbol for the soul.

We should note that by the term "evolution of the soul" we mean a process of a parallel and symmetrical evolution of both the soul and the mind, which results in the appearance of a new element generated as an amalgam of these two; this new element is the SPIRIT.

This is the evolutionary state that was achieved by the soul of Er, a soul capable of controlling, according to the myth, even the process of death. Now the potential to evolve, in turn, the cultivation of human *spirit* is a major goal for the entire Greek philosophy, perhaps even its raison d'être. Of course, the cultivation of spirit has assumed several different names, depending on the particular teachings of each philosopher:

Hesiod[1] calls it metaphorically "holy wedding", the Aristotelian philosophers "*technosis* of the mind", Pythagoras "Aphrodisia", Heraclitus "*antixoun sympheron*" ("difficult interest"), Empedocles presents it as the coupling of *philotes* ("attraction" or "love") and *neikos* ("repulsion" or "strife") in the case of human beings.

Thus, we realize that even in the first lines of the ancient text there is encoded in a truly masterly manner the fundamental relation between the MIND (Alcinous) and the SOUL (*alkimos*), as well as the future creation of the SPIRIT of Er. This means that we are supposed to have understood by now that the Phaiacians of old, like our contemporary society, were extremely advanced in their mental evolution and technology, and they had managed to achieve marvellous technological feats. However, this fact was not capable of leading them to prosperity, because they apparently lacked the aptitude to utilize and exploit this technology in a proper and legitimate manner. On the contrary, they had come to the point of being captives of this technology; the modern reader can reflect on the Homeric passage about their ships moving by themselves and going wherever the ships wanted, as compared to the modern concept of a computer-controlled autopilot, or with the resistance to the technology of autopiloted cars because of the "freedom of driving" sentiment. In other words, technology tends to di-

---

1. Ancient Greek poetry in general had strong philosophical tendencies and the epic poet Hesiod, like Homer, demonstrates a deep interest in a wide range of philosophical issues. See Allen, William (2006): *Tragedy and the Early Greek Philosophical Tradition, A Companion to Greek Tragedy*, Blackwell Publishing.

rect the human life and not vice-versa. It is an indisputable fact that nowadays humans are more and more dependent on their technology, while they are not able to further improve to an equal extent their well-being by making proper use of this super-technology.

This situation arises naturally when the technological progress of a civilisation is not accompanied by an equivalent evolution of the souls; when humans do not possess the spirit that could assign meaning and value to the existence and usage of the super-evolved technology.

Hence, we conclude that the myth of Er is an extremely timely text, because it begins by describing a situation we increasingly experience nowadays, without having realized it. Today we use technology by default, without thinking about it, wrongly believing that we are led towards a supposed progress, while, on the contrary, we are following the example of the Phaiacians and the most probable outcome is that sooner or later we will be led to the exile of an irrational and unbalanced society, a society possessing a technological civilisation but not *ethos* (morality). The most probable result of this is a corresponding disaster, which will be caused by wars, ecological destruction and/or a series of economic crises that will send people literally into "exile" like the Phaiacians, as people migrate in order to find employment.

HUMAN PROGRESS

TECHNOLOGICAL
CIVILISATION

CULTIVATION
OF SOUL

Humans can achieve progress only when their technological civilisation, and more generally their intellectual virtues, walk in parallel with the corresponding "cultivation" (= culture) of the soul (moral virtues), which unfortunately is not the case with our modern civilisation.

A situation in which the whole humanity is determined by its intake of only the intellectual virtues, and it does not cultivate in parallel the moral virtues, could be extremely dangerous. It is exactly at this point where the great problem of our civilisation resides, for the intellectual virtues are the ones which can be taught in schools and universities, while unfortunately the moral virtues are not taught, only cultivated by means of a meditative life that today is for most persons minimal or nonexistent. This is the serious ailment of our society; the lack of morality decomposes the notion of civilisation itself. And this is exactly the topic examined by Plato's *Republic*, the last part of which is the myth of Er.

Plato researches the issue of how a worthy statesman could emerge, a person who would be able, by setting the adequate laws, to develop the moral standing of the citizens. Otherwise we cannot talk about civilisation, nor about true evolution, only about a dangerous technological development and an ailing facet of the society.[2]

We should realize (better late than never) that this is most probably the greatest offer of Greek philosophy to the human race, because we observe that this aspect of human nature has not been understood and accessed as much as it should have been.

To this direction, we can once again employ the capability of the Greek language to indicate some truths through the similarity of words; in this case, the Greek words NOUS = mind, NAUS = ship and NAOS = temple are combinations of the same five letters, all starting with N. Which means that, from the moment the Phaiacians do not control the route and the function of their automated ships, this indicates a lack of control over the function of their own minds. We should understand this metaphor of the vessels as the representation of an uncontrollable mind left free to take its own initiatives and to direct the body to act at its will, following certain instincts, without feeling the need to seek even the slightest moral approval by the soul of its owner.

A person who has not cultivated the moral virtues, which are the only ones that could place barriers and internal inhibitions in the way he faces his life, is ready to "walk over corpses" in order to satisfy his ego. No matter how powerful or significant he is regarded by the modern society, which probably uses him even as an exemplar, by the ancient Greek philosophical standards he is not even considered human, being characterized as a puppet or slave.

---

2. A similar view is expressed by Sigmund Freud in his book *Das Unbehagen in der Kultur* (1930, Engl. translation *Civilization and Its Discontents*, London: Penguin, 2002).

In other words, even a super-scientist who has not culti-vated his moral essence remains at the inferior human level and acts like an automaton. According to the Greek philos-ophy, there are three evolutionary stages from which every human wanting to advance to a higher level must pass.

First stage	Second stage	Third stage
Humanoid, puppet, slave	Human	"Self-human"
Bipolar state	Approach of *mesotes*	God-like state

The first evolutionary stage pertains to the acquisition of only the intellectual virtues: wisdom, prudence and careful-ness, which are acquired through learning.

The second evolutionary stage pertains to the cultiva-tion and development of the 12 moral virtues, which are acquired through initiation.

The third evolutionary stage pertains to the completion of the human destination, that is to the achievement of its *entelecheia* (the convergence of actuality and potentiality) or of a God-like state.

The first stage of evolution according to Aristotle is called a "humanoid" or "two-legged creature"; the corresponding term used by Plato is *anthropiskos* (little human), while Py-thagoras uses the word *andrapodon* (slave from war, pup-pet). At this first stage are all persons who, irrespective of the knowledge they have acquired in their lives and their academic degrees, have not made even a first small step that could lead their souls towards the understanding and the application of the virtue of justice.

Plato's *Republic* as a whole addresses exactly this great

issue of the acquisition and function of the virtue of justice, which can be conquered only through the cultivation and the application of the moral virtues by the human soul.

Using as a criterion the application or not of the virtue of justice in our lives, we can bring ourselves to the point of knowing whether the path we follow leads us towards our *entelecheia*; if, in other words, we keep in pace with the application of the universal laws of justice.

Because from the moment a person begins to check the actions that support his or her activities of everyday life and finds that they are not governed by the virtue of justice, he or she should be able to understand that this is the wrong path. If we find ourselves in such a position, we must realize that there is an absolute need to disconnect immediately the autopilot that controls our mental functions and to take over the control of our "vessel" ourselves, using the tiller or the ship's wheel, the oars and the compass in order to be able to correct its course. An uncontrolled course is the result of an unevolved person and will lead without doubt to destructive results. This act of disconnecting the auto-pilot and taking over once again the control of our ship is called the restoration of the Free Will; unfortunately, very few people understand its meaning and are thus able to ac-tivate it.

Plato, then, makes clear from the beginning that what in-terests him in the Myth of Er is not, in any case, the kind of humans who have evolved only intellectually, like Alcinous; because these persons, from the moment they operate through the "autopilot", do not really decide themselves about their actions, they cannot be just and hence they are almost totally unevolved, as far as their personal evolution is concerned. A consequence of this, according to Plato, is that their soul still needs many future reincarnations in order to manage to acquire the valuable experiences that are necessary to guide them towards the correct course, as instruments of "navigation".

Instead, the philosopher wants to study the case of a man who had been an *alkimos* warrior and succeeded in advancing sufficiently the evolution of his soul and will. Of a man who had the power to control the movements of his "ship", to deactivate the "autopilot" of the mind and to assume the demanding task of navigation himself, even using his muscular power for rowing, but at the same time a man armed with the necessary knowledge that would allow him to read the compass and thus to be able to reach safely his personal NAOS, to arrive at his personal Ithaca.

Why is this high level of soul evolution expressed through a soldier? Er is a positive example or a metaphor of the *hoplite*, the citizen-soldier of ancient Greek city-states (once again, the anagram appears: OPLITIS = hoplite, POLITIS = free citizen): he is the person who has been trained in his life to fight, in a disciplined and effective way, in order to be able to choose by himself the course he decides he must follow, and not to leave the society or the State to direct him where *they* want.

So, as a first conclusion, we could set the principle that we should not be interested solely in the development of a powerful mind, i.e. the acquisition of academic knowledge alone, because the mind that records and processes this knowledge is susceptible to aging, sickness, injury and death. What we should be interested in is primarily the perspective of the development of a healthy soul, because the soul is immortal and for this reason it is vital to us to have it strong and healthy, and to keep it this way, so that after our death it will follow a path similar to that of the soul of Er. For, as it is indicated later in the text, a healthy soul is far superior and far more powerful than any available or future technology. In other words, a soul controlled only and fully by the cognition of an *alkimos* person has the full and cognitive responsibility about the evolutionary path it decides to follow.

The force of this soul can overpower any technology, since, according to the Platonic text, this soul can subdue and revert even the inevitable event of death!

For this reason, Plato, reaching the final part of his *Republic*, announces that now he will not describe to us the possibilities opened by the development of a technological civilisation that could arise in a state, but that instead he will focus on the development of the spiritual power that can and must be developed by the citizens, if the latter wish to act like heroes, in other words to follow the example of Er.

Therefore, we should learn the identity of this hero, Er, which Plato decides to denote through a myth, in other words encrypted or encoded. In this manner, Plato inserts Er into the sphere of the highest philosophy, which is the supreme secret of Greek mythology.

Our personal work here should be to "de-myth", i.e. to decode and interpret correctly this myth, attempting as a starting point to elucidate the identity of this mysterious soldier with the peculiar name: Er.

Without a doubt, the name of Er is not mentioned any-where else by Plato, or by any other ancient writer. In our attempt to decode his name, we should reside on the fact that his basic characteristic mentioned in the text is that he is a soldier. Which means that he is a person who has learned to give and to win personal fights; a man who has acquired the spiritual power of the free will and thus has conquered the right to follow consciously a particular tac-tic and a particular course, in contrast with the ships of the Phaiacians, which function without cognitive thought, be-ing directed by external forces.

We can probably extract hidden information from within the name of Er if we observe its declension: Its nominative case is ER, its genitive case is EROS and its accusative case is ERA.

The accusative case is identical in the Greek alphabet with the name of goddess Hera, the wife of Zeus; this god-dess is associated in both Greek mythology and Greek phi-losophy with the notion of the soul.

As for the genitive case, we have already observed that EROS is easily anagrammatised to the genitive case ROES of the noun *roé* = flux or flow. Let us examine this in more detail.

In the science of physics, the flux (also *roé* in modern Greek) is a most general notion, a concept describing the flow of a physical property in space, usually denoting an observed continuous motion of matter or energy through space. In a more restricted sense, it is a synonym of flow, having to do with the continuous macroscopic motion of fluid matter (gases and especially liquids), being the basic notion in fluid dynamics. The flux as a flow of energy is mostly associated with electromagnetism, as electric flux, magnetic flux and Poynting flux (electromagnetic energy flux). The flux lies at the foundation of the field concept, one of the most basic concepts in theoretical physics. All kinds of radiation can be associated with an energy flux; light is just a form of electromagnetic radiation and as such it is associated with the Poynting flux. In addition to pure physics, there is the flow or flux of air masses in meteorology. Other sciences, such as biology and optics, also use the concept of flux. Finally, in a more abstract form, the term has been borrowed by applied mathematics. Thus, the notion of ROES describes the concept of the continuous motion of matter or energy, which is of interest for our attempt to examine all possible aspects of the secret identity of Er.

It is an interesting coincidence that the name with which Plato called the hero of his myth can be anagrammatised in a very simple and easy way in Greek, to refer to a specialized scientific term. In the following chapters, we will see that the notion of flux could be associated with the unknown functions of our soul, after its separation from its material body, according to Plato's own beliefs.

Therefore, in order to elucidate the functions of our soul according to Plato, which are of course undetectable by our senses or by scientific instruments, we could compare them to scientific concepts associated with the observable phenomena of energy flux, which not only can be observed but also measured. This is probably the reason that the soul in classical philosophy was associated with the classical element of "water" and thus, indirectly, with the concept of flow. Even in the modern esoteric philosophy that associates the soul with energy (albeit in a sense only loosely connected to the strict scientific definition of energy), it could be easily connected, according to our scheme, with the physics of the Poynting flux or of the electric flux.

As a final conclusion, we could hypothesize that, when the soul of Er departed from his body, it followed a course as a flux, which is totally unknown and unique, until it returned to the apparently dead body from which it began its journey.

However, not only the Greek declensions of the name of Er with their impressive connections can reveal important information about the hero, but also two other elements of his identity can be interpreted to reveal encoded beliefs.

According to the text, Er is a descendant of Pamphylus and probably lived in Armenia. The word PAMPHYLOS (this is the original Greek form) is a composite, from the words PAN = all and PHYLON = race, tribe or sex. This hints that Er is not a solitary or infrequent case, but on the contrary it exemplifies the path followed by all souls after the death of their material body, a path our myth is set to reveal to us. In other words, ALL the reincarnated souls on planet Earth, irrespectively of the race, tribe or sex their bodies belong to, irrespectively of their apparent differentiations, from the moment they will lose their material body, they will follow a common and absolutely well-defined path that will lead them until the moment of their judgement.

The homeland of Er, ARMENIA, hints exactly at the evolution of the human soul after death. The Greek verb *armenizo* means "to travel aboard a sailing ship." This leads to the interpretation that the reincarnated soul has to focus in learning how to use the "sails", the "tiller", and the "compass" of the ship-body-mind, in order to have its absolute control and not to use the "autopilot". Thus, by relying exclusively on our own forces, we (in Plato's belief "we" means our souls) can safely reach our destination. That is to say, we must not "let ourselves to a life" in which our mind will just follow the directions that will receive mostly subconsciously by its wider environment; on the contrary, we should have the power to intervene and to determine its course based on the needs of its own soul.

We must comprehend that only in such a case we really use the free will we are equipped with; in all other cases we just have the illusion that the decisions we take are our own, which is not true as it will be shown later.

Let us not forget that Athena, the goddess of the intellectual virtue of wisdom, but also of the moral virtue of *sophrosyne* (prudence) was the one who offered to Jason, the leader of the Argonauts, the rudder of the ship Argo, so that he would have been able to steer the ship to the correct course at any moment. This is what the ships of the Phaiacians lacked, as we have seen; in addition to not having oars (the analog of using an advanced propulsion technology, something that is certainly a positive element), the Phaiacian ships also lacked rudders, in other words they lacked a strategy of redetermining their destination, their target, and even the general direction they should follow, which is of course a negative element.

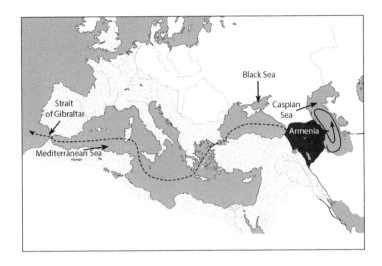

On the other hand, we should by no means exclude from our examination the special geographic location of Armenia, the homeland of Er. We can readily realize that it lies at a strategic point of our planet, between the Caspian Sea and the Black Sea.

The Caspian Sea is the largest lake in the world by area; despite its large size, it is enclosed by land. On the contrary, the Black Sea (known to the Greeks as the *Euxeinos Pontos*) belongs to the real "seas"; it might be considered "closed" from almost all sides, yet it has an exit, which, although extremely narrow, can be located and followed by a sailing ship that knows how to use a compass to select and determine its course.

This exit of the Black Sea, far from being a nondescript location, consists of the famous triad of the Bosporus Strait, the Sea of Marmara and the Strait of the Dardanelles. The latter is near the Homeric Troy and connects all the above to the Aegean Sea and the wider Mediterranean Sea. From there, any ship can pass the Strait of Gibraltar, known in the ancient world as the "Pillars of Hercules", and sail in the open Ocean.

Hence, the homeland of Er lies at a geographic position from which one could be lured by two distinct watery bodies. Here is hidden still another metaphor: Our soul can also follow two different and quite distinct paths; let us not forget that a symbol for the soul in classical philosophy was the element of water.

If Er, residing in Armenia, wants to leave his land (an analog for the embodied state of the soul), he has two choices: Either he will sail in the Caspian Sea, or, following the opposite direction, he will sail in the Black Sea.

By selecting the former, he will not have an "escape exit", just the opportunity to circumnavigating the shores of this vast but closed lake, so inevitably he will return to the same point from where he started his trip. In the soul metaphor, the soul of Er would have in this case to be reincarnated.

However, if Er chooses the other direction and manages to sail in the Black Sea, then, by using properly the ship's wheel and with the adequate manoeuvres, he is offered the possibility of escape. In this case, he could travel as far away as the Atlantic Ocean. He would find himself in a totally different environment, which not only is unrestricted, but it can offer several distinct opportunities of sailing. In our analogy, the soul could follow the direction, that is its future reincarnation, of its own choice.

According to what Plato will reveal in the following sections of his text, in the first case, the one corresponding to the selection of the Caspian Sea, the next reincarnation of the soul will be totally determined by the three Moirai (the Fates). However, in the second case, that of the selection of the Black Sea, the whole process of the next reincarnation is an exclusive choice of the soul itself, which is influenced only partially by its Fate, since now its Free Will can function as well.

The latter is the case of Er, who, from the moment he appears as *alkimos*, has strengthened his soul to such a degree that now he can divert his course from following his Fate, because as we have seen, he has taken to a large extent his fate in his hands, since he sails his ship, his NAUS-NOUS (= mind), only with his own abilities, knowing how to use its oars, wheel and compass.

Beyond the sea routes, it would be a great omission if we did not mention the fact that in the region of Armenia there are also the Caucasus Mountains, on which, according always to the Greek mythology, was Prometheus bound.

The analogy that could be present here is that every human soul, from the moment it is embodied on planet Earth, can be compared to the bound Prometheus. For it is mandatorily coupled with the body and thus restricted within the narrow physical boundaries of the latter, in this small corner of the vast Universe, where, as long as it remains only mentally evolved, acquiring only scientific knowledge, it follows a compulsory, particular way of life, the one dictated by this knowledge in every time period.

In the specific case of Er, we should understand that this soldier represents "Prometheus Unbound", that play by the Greek poet Aeschylus, of which unfortunately only fragments survive (as if we should not learn how to untie ourselves and to be liberated from our restrictions, unless we use our own personal powers). However, we can conclude that probably this lost play was also a metaphor for the way our soul could be set free from the chains of its reincarnations, which keep it bound to the Earth. It would be a good guess that, if liberated, the soul would function as a "Prometheus the Fire-Bringer", i.e. it would proceed to the integration of its mind into spirit, or to the "holy wedding" of the soul and the mind, so that it would function both its poles in a cognitive way, and in this manner it would successfully enter the third evolutionary stage, becoming a "Self-human".

Therefore, what we should understand is that Armenia or the Caucasus Mountains, with their characteristic location between the Caspian Sea and the Black Sea, offer metaphorically the opportunity to the embodied soul to sail (*armenizo*) in either sea, depending on whether its free will is functioning or not.

In case the soul does not manage to assume the control of its ship's wheel, like Alcinous and the other Phaiacians, it will inevitably end up in the Caspian Sea, from where, not having a way to escape, it will obviously continue the repeating reincarnations on the planet Earth until it manages during a future life to become an *alkimos* from being an Alcinous.

In the opposite case, in which the soul has succeeded in assuming the control of its ship's wheel, like Er or Jason, who had Athena as their ally, the soul can throw its ship in the Black Sea, thus breaking the cycle of its inevitable reincarnations, since it now possesses both the strategy and the wisdom (as expressions of its free will) to lead its ship out in the open seas.

As a conclusion, we realize that through all the above encodings, with which Plato so artfully integrated the identity of Er, the great philosopher actually wants to describe the secret path, the "flow" our soul has to follow after the death of the material body it ensouls. In other words, an esoteric interpretation that could be our basis for decoding the title "The Myth of Er" is the following:

"THE SECRET FLOW or PATH TAKEN BY OUR SOUL BE-TWEEN DEATH AND REINCARNATION"

Having a first glimpse of the content of this myth-metaphor and of the manner in which we have to decode every significant piece of information contained in the text, we can now proceed and follow step-by-step this mystical and unknown itinerary of our soul during its journey in the universal ocean of its after-death wandering.

Chapter 2
DESCRIBING THE ROUTE OF THE SOUL
OF ER IN THE INVISIBLE WORLD

... ἔφη δέ, ἐπειδὴ οὗ ἐκβῆναι, τὴν ψυχὴν πορεύεσθαι [614c] μετὰ πολλῶν, καὶ ἀφικνεῖσθαι σφᾶς εἰς τόπον τινὰ δαιμόνιον, ἐν ᾧ τῆς τε γῆς δύ᾽ εἶναι χάσματα ἐχομένω ἀλλήλοιν καὶ τοῦ οὐρανοῦ αὖ ἐν τῷ ἄνω ἄλλα καταντικρύ. δικαστὰς δὲ μεταξὺ τούτων καθῆσθαι, οὕς, ἐπειδὴ διαδικάσειαν, τοὺς μὲν δικαίους κελεύειν πορεύεσθαι τὴν εἰς δεξιάν τε καὶ ἄνω διὰ τοῦ οὐρανοῦ, σημεῖα περιάψαντας τῶν δεδικασμένων ἐν τῷ πρόσθεν, τοὺς δὲ ἀδίκους τὴν εἰς ἀριστεράν τε καὶ κάτω, ἔχοντας καὶ τούτους ἐν τῷ ὄπισθεν σημεῖα πάντων ὧν [614d] ἔπραξαν. ἑαυτοῦ δὲ προσελθόντος εἰπεῖν ὅτι δέοι αὐτὸν ἄγγελον ἀνθρώποις γενέσθαι τῶν ἐκεῖ καὶ διακελεύοιντό οἱ ἀκούειν τε καὶ θεᾶσθαι πάντα τὰ ἐν τῷ τόπῳ. ὁρᾶν δὴ ταύτῃ μὲν καθ᾽ ἑκάτερον τὸ χάσμα τοῦ οὐρανοῦ τε καὶ τῆς γῆς ἀπιούσας τὰς ψυχάς, ἐπειδὴ αὐταῖς δικασθείη, κατὰ δὲ τὼ ἑτέρω ἐκ μὲν τοῦ ἀνιέναι ἐκ τῆς γῆς μεστὰς αὐχμοῦ τε καὶ κόνεως, ἐκ δὲ τοῦ ἑτέρου καταβαίνειν ἑτέρας ἐκ τοῦ [614e] οὐρανοῦ καθαράς.

ἔφη δέ, ἐπειδὴ οὗ ἐκβῆναι, τὴν ψυχὴν πορεύεσθαι μετὰ πολλῶν...

57

... So Er said that, after leaving his body, his soul followed a path along with many other souls...

The soul of Er left his body, but it was not totally separated from it, as it happened with all the other souls of the dead. In modern esoteric philosophy, there is the analogy of the "silver cord": during a similar out-of-body experience, the soul remains connected to the body through an ethereal substance. If this silver cord breaks, for any reason, then the person dies immediately and forever.

... καὶ ἀφικνεῖσθαι σφᾶς εἰς τόπον τινὰ δαιμόνιον...

... and they all together arrived at a mysterious place, where there are only higher beings of daemonic (ethereal) soul...

The use of the word "daemonic" should not mislead us, since it is one of those words the meaning of which has undergone a major alteration of its original Greek and Roman sense.

Plato himself gives us a definition of the word "daemon" in his dialogue *Cratylus*, where it explains it as "the knowledgeable one", citing an etymology from *daïmon*. Also, in his *Symposium*, he calls love "a great daemon". Hence, we should accept that the nature of this daemonic place is linked to the element of love, as well as with the elements of happiness and rest. In the funeral *acolouthia* or ceremony of the Orthodox Church, this place is characterized as *chloeros* (grassy), "where there is no pain, sorrow or sigh".

The element of love in daemons has to do with their role, which is to connect the inferior souls of humans with the divine souls. Using modern terminology, we could say that daemon is the "guardian angel".

Therefore, it should be understood that this "daemonic place" where the souls arrive after the death of their material bodies has entirely different conditions, characteristics and properties from the terrestrial conditions we experience for as long as out soul is reincarnated on planet Earth.

... ἐν ᾧ τῆς τε γῆς δύ' εἶναι χάσματα ἐχομένω ἀλλήλοιν...

... and where, being above the surface of the Earth, there are two voids or openings, an inferior and a superior one, which are interconnected..

This is a most important and interesting description of this daemonic region, which is defined by these two voids or openings that function as passageways for the souls, exactly because all these remain invisible for our bodily eyes and it is impossible to perceive them with our senses.

... καὶ τοῦ οὐρανοῦ αὖ ἐν τῷ ἄνω ἄλλα καταντικρύ.

The superior void touches the heaven and all the points

of these two voids are symmetrical to one another.

....

Until a few decades ago, these voids would be impossible to be interpreted by any reader of this text in association with any structure in the natural world. However, the advancements of the twentieth-century technology and science added new scientific knowledge, which offers us an intriguing analogy of the above description in the outer space near the Earth.

Modern space science knows nowadays that such symmetrical and interconnected voids or openings as the ones mentioned in this ancient text are formed by the presence of two wide toroidal rings, which curve over the entire surface of planet Earth with the exception of the polar regions.

These two rings are the famous **Van Allen radiation belts,** named after the American space scientist James A. Van Allen (1914-2006), whose instruments aboard the first U.S. artificial satellites (*Explorer 1* and *Explorer 3*) discovered them in early 1958, by measuring the density of the charged particles in various regions of space.

The geometry and the relative positions of these energy belts set with accuracy the boundaries of the two voids: the one void is formed between them and the other is formed between the inner Van Allen belt and the surface of the Earth, a close analogy with the Platonic text. The former void is the superior one, while the latter, which touches the surface of our planet, is the inferior one. Indeed, all points of these two void regions are symmetrical to one another. These can be called "voids" because they are relatively devoid of high-energy particles, which are forced to be concentrated in the interior of the Van Allen belts. The two voids are connected with the exterior outer space ("the heaven" of the ancient text) through the regions above the poles of the Earth.

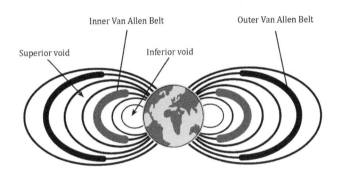

At this point we begin to realize that, in addition to the advanced metaphysical knowledge of Plato and his penetrating insights regarding the invisible world, the great philosopher also makes very interesting guesses of aspects of the modern scientific knowledge, which were discovered as recently as half a century ago.

On the other hand, the word *chasmata* (= voids, openings) used by Plato in the ancient text can probably be interpreted as having a second, additional, meaning, in a kind of more subtle pun: It can be said that through this word Plato tries to communicate to us the fact that what is about to be said in the following part of the text consists of advanced knowledge, which will be *de facto* incomprehensible to uneducated persons. In other words, an additional interpretation of the word *chasmata* is that of "voids of knowledge"; today, this can apply to persons who do not possess knowledge of astronomy, astrophysics or space science and thus they find equally incomprehensible the pioneering revelations of modern science. Another analogy is the modern socio-scientific term "digital divide", which exists between the individuals who have access to, use of, or impact of information and communication technologies, and those who do not; or between the technologically literate persons, who take advantage of the capabilities of the new technologies, and those who for any reason did not follow a similar course.

If space science had not advanced to the levels achieved in the 20th century and we were at the state of knowledge that existed before 1958, it would be impossible to perceive the analogies between the path of the souls ascending to the Platonic heavens though "voids", and the characteristic two voids between the Earth and the far outer space, which are also characterized by symmetry.

Such analogies gave rise to the unconventional hypothesis that in ancient Greece there was available, at least to a few selected or "initiated" individuals, highly advanced scientific knowledge, including what are thought of as discoveries of the 20th century, such as the Van Allen radiation belts. The ancient Greek philosophers are thus said to know in every detail what modern science only began to discover in recent decades.

More fascinating similarities arise when we study more details about the Van Allen belts and how they can be related to the Platonic "soul paths".

Today we know that these belts consist of moving elementary particles, almost exclusively electrons and protons[3], which bear an electric charge; thus their motion produces electric FLUXES or currents, which reminds the notion of ROES we associated in the previous chapter with the genitive case of the name ER (EROS), as an "encoded" connection.

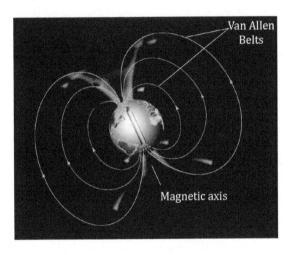

As we can see in the above images, the inner Van Allen belt is surrounded by the outer belt; together, they form two enormous toroidal rings that surround the globe of the Earth in azimuth (i.e. extending over all meridians) and curve over it in the sense of the latitude, leaving openings above the polar regions.

A very impressive and interesting fact about these belts is that they result from different natural processes; more

---

3. Strictly speaking, protons are not elementary, since they consist of quarks; however, quarks are never found free in nature.

specifically, it is generally understood that their particles originate from two different sources, one of which is the Sun and the other is associated with the extrasolar space:

The outer belt owes its existence to the flow of energetic particles from the Sun, known as the solar wind. Being electrically charged, these particles are trapped in the magnetic field of the Earth, since all charged particles that move inside a magnetic field experience a force with a direction perpendicular to their motion, and so they gyrate and move along magnetic field lines. As the particles encounter regions of larger density of magnetic field lines, (i.e. stronger field) their north-south speed component is slowed and can be reversed, thus reflecting the particles. This causes the particles to bounce back and forth between the Earth's poles, remaining inside the Van Allen belt. Globally, the motion of these trapped particles is chaotic. The highest density of particles in the outer Van Allen belt, mainly electrons, is located at an altitude (height) of about 16,000 kilometres (km) above the Earth's equator. The outer belt extends typically from an altitude of about 13,000 km to about 60,000 km above the surface of the Earth.

On the contrary, the inner Van Allen belt, which consists mainly of protons and electrons, apparently owes its existence to the decay of so-called "albedo" neutrons, which are themselves the result of cosmic-ray collisions in the upper atmosphere. The highest density of particles in the inner belt is located at an altitude of approximately 3,200 km above the surface of our planet. The belt itself extends from an altitude of about 1,000 km to about 6,000 km above the surface; however, when the solar activity is stronger or in geographical regions such as the South Atlantic Anomaly, the inner boundary may go down to roughly 200 km above the surface.

We should also know that solar wind particles, like the ones that compose the outer Van Allen belt, although themselves are invisible to the eye, they can be made indirectly visible at the polar regions of the Earth, by forming one of the most beautiful and impressive natural spectacles one could see from our planet: The aurora, or the northern and southern lights. This phenomenon was associated, as it should be expected, with ancient myths and traditions of many tribes and nations, which offered various explanations. Nowadays, after the exponential growth of scientific knowledge during the previous century, we know that it is a natural phenomenon, originating from increased solar activity, when the solar wind becomes so powerful that it penetrates the region where the Earth's magnetic field dominates (the magnetosphere, as it is called) and reaches the outer atmosphere of the Earth. Then, its high-energy particles strike the molecules and atoms of the higher atmosphere and ionize them, separating their electrons from them; when these electrons recombine with the atoms, a light of characteristic colour is produced, depending on the element; e.g. oxygen produces a beautiful cold green colour in middle heights and a red colour higher on.

It is very interesting that Aristotle in his work *Meteorologica* (Book I, 5) describes the aurora phenomenon and attempts to explain it, although it is seldom seen from the low latitude of Greece; this is another demonstration of the high level of awareness about nature and natural phenomena achieved by the ancient Greek philosophers.

A display of aurora borealis (the "Northern Lights"): a curtain that hides the mystical path of our soul according to Plato.

Δικαστὰς δὲ μεταξὺ τούτων καθῆσθαι, οὕς, ἐπειδὴ διαδικάσειαν,...

In the place between these two voids [or: where the two voids connect] were sitting judges, who, after they judge about the future path to be followed by the souls of the dead,...

Once again, Plato attempts here to relate specific locations to the path the human souls follow after death. He appears to know that such locations do exist in space. A most fitting analogy in accordance with the above description would be the edges of the Van Allen radiation belts above the polar regions of the Earth, where the aurora forms. In such a place Plato believes that reside the judges of our souls. These are the only regions where the two voids meet, and hence one could imagine that they could have some kind of contact and communication.

The reader now begins to understand the unknown mystical itinerary a soul has to follow from the moment it leaves its material body. That is to say, when we "die" our soul exits our material body, which up to then was vitalizing, and is transferred to certain physically invisible region, where the two voids connect; in our analogy, above the northern or the southern polar region. In other words, we should understand that after the death of our material body our soul remains for a certain time period at a "hovering" state between Earth and heaven, waiting for its hour of judgement.

The judges reside at the region where the two voids merge, presumably because from there they can decide the appropriate direction each soul should follow after their judgement and send it directly there; this direction would, of course, correspond to the extent each soul had practiced the virtue of justice as long as it was reincarnated on planet Earth.

As it is known from the Greek mythology, in front of the entrance, in the forecourt of the palace of Hades and Persephone are seated the three judges of the Underworld: Minos, Rhadamanthus, and Aeacus. Additionally, at the same location there was a sanctuary devoted to Hecate, where three roads meet (trivium).

If the forecourt of the residence of Hades could be correlated with the Van Allen belts, then his palace itself could be correlated with the near (visible from the Earth) side of the Moon.

This *trivium* clearly pertains to the future itinerary of the soul, which, as we will see in the following, is forced to follow one of three distinct paths, depending on the result of the verdict.

... τοὺς μὲν δικαίους κελεύειν πορεύεσθαι τὴν εἰς δεξιάν τε καὶ ἄνω διὰ τοῦ οὐρανοῦ,...

... they order the [souls of the] righteous to journey to the right and upwards through the heaven,...

Thus, according to the verdict of the judges, the souls of the righteous persons can proceed and enter what in our analogy is the outer Van Allen belt. This means that probably certain righteous souls could be led by some manner even to higher heavenly places, something that, as we will see later, obviously happened to the soul of Er.

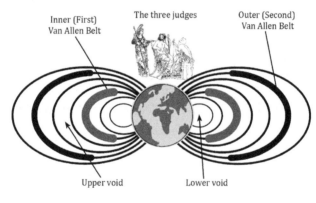

... σημεῖα περιάψαντας τῶν δεδικασμένων ἐν τῷ πρόσθεν,...

... after they attach signs [of all the judged important events of their lives] to them in front of the judgement passed upon them...

These higher heavenly places correspond to what other ancient Greek writers call "Fortunate Isles" or, more literally, "Isles of the Blessed"; however, the Platonic heavens correspond[4] to the sphere of the fixed stars, that is of the constellations we observe in the night sky. According to Greek mythology, the Isles of the Blessed were reserved for those who had chosen to be reincarnated thrice, and managed to be judged as especially pure enough to gain entrance to the Elysian Fields all three times. These Fields, in turn, have been interpreted as a part of the far side of the Moon, which is invisible from the Earth.

... τοὺς δὲ ἀδίκους τὴν εἰς ἀριστεράν τε καὶ κάτω,...

But the other souls, being judged as unrighteous, are ordered to journey to the left and downward,...

Obviously, these souls of the unrighteous persons must repeat the process of the reincarnation, until they, too, manage to serve the virtue of justice. To this end, they enter the region that is the analogue of the inner or lower Van Allen belt. There they will drink the "water of oblivion", thus forgetting the memories that are associated with their previous life; this process is repeated prior to each reincarnation.

---

4. Émile Bréhier: *La philosophie de Plotin*, Paris: Boivin, 1928; pp. 28-29

... ἔχοντας καὶ τούτους ἐν τῷ ὄπισθεν σημεῖα πάντων ὧν ἔπραξαν.

... also wearing behind signs of all their important actions [which force them to return back to Earth for a new reincarnation].

These "signs" correspond to what today we would recognise as the karma of Hinduism and other Asian religions. This list of deeds and misdeeds, a kind of algebraic summation of good (positive) and bad (negative) behaviour during a lifetime, marks the soul and determines its evolutionary path. In other words, they are the critical factor that defines the conditions under which a given soul is obliged to be reincarnated.

We can observe here that the judgment of the souls is inevitably accompanied by an event of the highest importance: the future path our soul will follow, as indicated by the words "in front" and "behind".

If the forward path is followed, this means that the particular soul has been judged capable of successfully completing the cycle of its reincarnations and now it has, as we will see, two options, after passing to the region that corresponds to the outer or upper Van Allen belt: It can either sever its connection to the terrestrial environment and migrate to the Elysian Fields and to the Isles of the Blessed, or it can return to the Earth, where it can freely continue its evolution to perfection, which proceeds along with the human *entelecheia* and the purpose of human life.

So the entrance of the soul to the region corresponding

to the outer Van Allen belt proves that during its previous reincarnation the soul chose the path to evolution and succeeded in following it.

If, on the other hand, the soul is forced to follow the backward path, this means that the particular soul did not evolve sufficiently during its previous reincarnation and has to repeat once more the process of reincarnation.

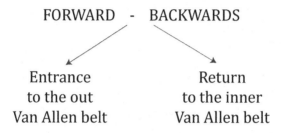

FORWARD - BACKWARDS

Entrance	Return
to the out	to the inner
Van Allen belt	Van Allen belt

Ἑαυτοῦ δὲ προσελθόντος εἰπεῖν ὅτι δέοι αὐτὸν ἄγγελον ἀνθρώποις γενέσθαι τῶν ἐκεῖ...

So when Er himself was transferred to this region [of judgement], they [= the judges] told him that he should become a messenger to mankind, to inform them about the existence of that world and about what takes place there.

Here we are told that Er, during this out-of-body experience he had, is granted the capability and opportunity to act as god Hermes (Mercury), the messenger of the Olympian gods.

This passage actually connects the revelations of the

Myth of Er to the initiation to Hermeticism, the religious, philosophical, and esoteric tradition based upon writings attributed to Hermes Trismegistus ("Thrice Great"), a combination of the Greek god Hermes and the Egyptian god Thoth. The initiation to Hermeticism remains today largely unknown.

... καὶ διακελεύοιντό οἱ ἀκούειν τε καὶ θεᾶσθαι πάντα τὰ ἐν τῷ τόπῳ.

Thus, they decided to charge him to give ear and to observe everything that happens in that place [of daemons], so that he would subsequently communicate them to humans. (Since they decided that his soul had the right to return to the same body.)

....

We understand from this passage that the power of these judges (probably the three judges of Hades, the Underworld) is enormous. The future path of our soul according to Plato depends on their verdict, i.e. whether each soul is considered worthy to interrupt the cycle of reincarnations and to disconnect from the terrestrial environment in order to go forth and evolve even further, or it is considered fit for more reincarnations, returning back to the prison of some material body on the Earth.

Ὁρᾶν δὴ ταύτῃ μὲν καθ' ἑκάτερον τὸ χάσμα τοῦ οὐρανοῦ τε καὶ τῆς γῆς ἀπιούσας τὰς ψυχάς, ἐπειδὴ αὐταῖς δικασθείη,...

And so Er said that there he saw [according to what the judges had decided to allow him] clearly, by each void of heaven and earth, the souls departing after judgement had been passed upon them;

In other words, when the souls are released from their material body in order to be led to the place of their judgement, they are channelled through these two voids or openings. After their judgement, they enter one of the two regions we parallel to the Van Allen belts.

This analogy can also be used for the well-known essay of Plutarch (in his *Moralia* collection) entitled "On the Face Which Appears in the Orb of the Moon", where he mentions the "diamond-shodden columns", a description that easily reminds to us the shining image of aurora in dark skies.

... κατὰ δὲ τὼ ἑτέρω ἐκ μὲν τοῦ ἀνιέναι ἐκ τῆς γῆς μεστὰς αὐχμοῦ τε καὶ κόνεως, ἐκ δὲ τοῦ ἑτέρου καταβαίνειν ἑτέρας ἐκ τοῦ οὐρανοῦ καθαράς.

and by the one void or opening, there came up from the earth souls full of dry dirt and dust, while from the other one there came down from heaven a second procession of souls clean and pure,

Here we realise that all the souls coming from dead bodies that are about to be judged, irrespective of their future judgement and of their subsequent itinerary, are all unclean and dusty. On the other side, all the souls coming down from heavens are perfectly clean; some of these souls, however, will go down to Earth through the first void in order to be reincarnated. Let us rephrase the situation in terms of the Van Allen belt analogy:

Some souls come from the Earth, they get judged and then they are directed to the inner Van Allen belt, from which they immediately return to Earth, since they have not undergone yet the required evolution. These souls are full of dirt and dust during both their ascent to the inner Van Allen belt and their descent to Earth to be reincarnated.

Now, there are the other souls, the ones that have managed to evolve during their stay on Earth, and hence they are granted the opportunity to enter the outer Van Allen belt. These souls can also return to Earth to be reincarnated if they wish, but even in this case they are cleansed, because in the outer belt they are purified by some way.

This means that there are two categories of souls getting reincarnated in our world: those who evolve and return cleansed, and those who have not evolved at all and continue to return "filthy". This view has been used to explain the great variety that characterizes the quality and the behaviour of the human souls.

We realise once again from the above that one could theorise equally well that the Platonic text refers to advanced metaphysical knowledge and that it alludes to advanced scientific knowledge (space science). As we saw, the author reveals the existence of twin voids or openings in the sky, in complete analogy to the two Van Allen belts. Remember that solar wind particles, like the ones that compose the outer Van Allen belt, produce the phenomenon of aurora (northern lights or southern lights). Aurora was called by the aboriginal Canadian tribe Cree the "Dance of the Spirits". Even more to the point, the Aboriginal Australian tribe Ngarrindjeri of South Australia referred to auroras seen over Kangaroo Island as the campfires of souls in the "Land of the Dead"; aboriginal people in southwest Queensland believed that the auroras were the fires of the "Oola Pikka", ghostly spirits who spoke to the people through auroras, and that messages of ancestors were transmitted through these strange variable lights. The aboriginal tribe Chipewyan of Western Canada believed that the northern lights were the souls of their departed friends dancing in the sky, and when the lights shined the brightest it meant that their deceased friends were very happy.[5]

A particularly Greek mythological feature in the Platonic description is the existence of the three judges of Hades and the paths (trivium) followed by the souls, depending on their qualitative evolution. However, up to this point we have discovered only the two of these paths. Since the judges are also three, there should be a third path, so that there would be complete agreement between the number of the judges and the number of the paths.

Well, it is quite impressive that as recently as in February 2013, about half a century after the discovery of the origi-

---

5. Hearne, Samuel (1958): *A Journey to the Northern Ocean: A journey from Prince of Wales' Fort in Hudson's Bay to the Northern Ocean in the years 1769, 1770, 1771, 1772*. Richard Glover (ed.). Toronto: The MacMillan Company of Canada; pp. 221–222.

nal two Van Allen belts, a third radiation belt, consisting of high-energy ultrarelativistic charged particles, was reported to be discovered by NASA's "Van Allen Probes", two unmanned spacecraft.

The twin Van Allen Probes, affectionately called "Van" and "Allen", were launched on August 30, 2012 aboard a single Atlas V rocket, and they are equipped with specialized instrument suites, which allowed scientists to collect information about the radiation of the belts in unprecedented detail.

This new information, in particular the data from the Relativistic Electron Proton Telescope (REPT) of the Energetic Particle, Composition, and Thermal Plasma Suite (ECT) aboard the second one of these probes, led for the first time to the complete imaging of particle densities and energies into each small region of the outer Van Allen belt, where all previous measurements offered only a vague image. And the results were truly impressive. First of all, the scientists discovered that the width of the belts could extend further away into space than previously known. However, the really fascinating new discovery was the Van Allen radiation belts are not always two, since there is a third, unknown up to now, belt, which can alternatively appear and disappear. It was stated that this third belt is generated when a mass coronal ejection is created by the Sun. It has been represented as a separate creation, which splits the outer Van Allen belt, like a knife, on its outer side, and exists separately as a storage container for a month's time, before merging once again with the outer belt. The unusual stability of this third, transient belt has been explained as due to a "trapping" by the Earth's magnetic field of ultrarelativistic particles as they are lost from the second, traditional outer belt. While the outer belt is highly variable owing to interactions with the atmosphere of the Earth, the ultrarelativistic particles of the third belt are thought to not scatter into the atmosphere, as they are too energetic to interact with atmospheric waves at low latitudes. This absence of scattering and the trapping allows them to persist for a long time, finally only being destroyed by an unusual event, such as an interplanetary shock wave from the Sun, which actually swept it away in the case observed, about a month after its creation.

In our analogy with the paths followed by the souls, we thought of the Van Allen belts as the forecourt of the palace of Hades and Persephone, the palace itself being located on the near (visible) side of the Moon, also known as "meadows of Persephone". We know that the outer Van Allen belts is produced by the same agent that forms the aurora; and the Greek word for the northern lights, SELAS, has the same root as SELENE, the Moon.

Now, we could conclude that the existence of the Van Allen radiation belts is intimately connected to the existence of the phenomenon of life on planet Earth. It is true that in the real Universe the presence of a global and sufficiently strong magnetic field maintained by a planet creates such radiation belts by channelling the charged particles of the solar or stellar wind, protecting at the same time the surface and all living creatures on it from these same high-energy particles that could expose this life to harmful radiation levels.

In other words, the presence of radiation belts could be a first indication of the existence of life on the surface of a given planet. With modern technology, we could very easily detect by using the suitable instruments whether a planet has such belts.

Extending our analogy of the Platonic text, we could say that, when the soul is reincarnated on the Earth, its carrier is the body, while when it is separated from its body, then its carrier becomes some high-energy charged particle inside a Van Allen radiation belt, possibly one of those that produce the aurora, as in the beliefs of the aboriginal tribes mentioned. When the members of these tribes were observing the awe-inspiring spectacle of an aurora, they had actually an additional reason to feel awe, since by looking at it they looked at a vast number of souls. According to Plato, all these souls are waiting to be reincarnated on our planet.

Still another Greek wordplay is in store for this aspect of the analogy: the genitive case of the word SELAS is SE-LAOS. Hence, we realise that "inside" the *selas* there is a LAOS, which means a large crowd of people, a "nation" of souls. The souls in the ancient Greek tradition originate from the Sun, just like the particles causing the aurora, since they are particles of the solar wind, which comes from the Sun. Moreover, SE in Greek is the accusative case of the pronoun "you".

According, then, to the latest discoveries, we could understand the correlation of the path of the souls with the Van Allen radiation belts and their function as following:

The inner or lower belt is correlated with the "lower" souls of humans, or even of animals; all these souls need to be reincarnated many more times, without having the right to choose their next life.

The outer or higher belt is correlated with the "higher" souls of humans; these fall into one of two distinct subcategories:

In the first subcategory belong the souls needing to be reincarnated, although they are already evolved, in order to complete their evolution. However, these souls possess the right to choose what their next reincarnation will be (as we will see in the following chapters) and they remain in the meadows of Persephone, until the moment (probably the moment of an eclipse of the Sun) they will be transferred to Earth.

In the second subcategory belong the completely evolved souls. These souls do not need to return to the Earth; they remain in the celestial meadows for only seven days, in order to be connected with their higher "self". Subsequently, these souls, having been connected with their superior self, become detached from the outer Van Allen belt and they form the third belt, because according to the Fate they have to follow a different path of non-incarnation.

This would be the mythical reason why the two traditional Van Allen belts are permanent, since there are always souls inside them, while the third belt is transient, since the souls it contains are carried simultaneously as a mass to the same destination, and not one-by-one to different bodies.

Nowadays, there are many testimonies of out-of-body experiences. There is a common element in them: Those who experience this state report that they appear to enter a tunnel towards a light, where conditions of absolute calm and serenity prevail. After the revelations of Er, we could suggest the analogy that this illuminated tunnel corresponds to the second void, which is surrounded by the two Van Allen belts, or by two "curtains" of aurora.

However, most testimonies of out-of-body experiences end at this point, since the souls are ordered to return to their embodied existence back on the Earth. On the contrary, the soul of Er examined in the Platonic text receives the order to continue, so that it will reveal to us the unknown route of the souls in the invisible world. Hence, we realise once more that the value of this ancient text is incalculable, because the information that is about to be disclosed has never been revealed before!

Chapter 3
THE MYTH OF ANDROGYNOUS
HUMANS AND THE HOLY FESTIVAL

Καὶ τὰς ἀεὶ ἀφικνουμένας ὥσπερ ἐκ πολλῆς πορείας φαίνεσθαι ἥκειν, καὶ ἀσμένας εἰς τὸν λειμῶνα ἀπιούσας οἷον ἐν πανηγύρει κατασκηνᾶσθαι, καὶ ἀσπάζεσθαί τε ἀλλήλας ὅσαι γνώριμαι, καὶ πυνθάνεσθαι τάς τε ἐκ τῆς γῆς ἡκούσας παρὰ τῶν ἑτέρων τὰ ἐκεῖ καὶ τὰς ἐκ τοῦ οὐρανοῦ τὰ παρ' ἐκείναις. διηγεῖσθαι δὲ ἀλλήλαις τὰς [615a] μὲν ὀδυρομένας τε καὶ κλαούσας, ἀναμιμνῃσκομένας ὅσα τε καὶ οἷα πάθοιεν καὶ ἴδοιεν ἐν τῇ ὑπὸ γῆς πορείᾳ — εἶναι δὲ τὴν πορείαν χιλιέτη — τὰς δ' αὖ ἐκ τοῦ οὐρανοῦ εὐπαθείας διηγεῖσθαι καὶ θέας ἀμηχάνους τὸ κάλλος. τὰ μὲν οὖν πολλά, ὦ Γλαύκων, πολλοῦ χρόνου διηγήσασθαι.

Καὶ τὰς ἀεὶ ἀφικνουμένας ὥσπερ ἐκ πολλῆς πορείας φαίνεσθαι ἥκειν,...

There will always be [souls of the dead] arriving [to the higher void], and these will be now happy [that their time on Earth ended], since they appear to have suffered a great deal of hardship, similar to that of a long travel;...

There is a perennial paradox in the human stance about death. As long as we live, we normally do not want to die by any means, and we even make every possible effort in order to delay the moment of our death. However, if Plato is right, then after our death, and if our soul is judged worthy of ascending to the higher stage (in our natural parallel this is the outer Van Allen belt), we are glad that, at last, we died, after the great hardships and sorrows of a terrestrial reincarnation.

For Plato clearly indicates that the soul after death resides at a place of rest, from which it can enter the Elysian Fields and/or the "Isles of the Blessed", having passed from the *chloeros* (grassy) place of the "meadows of Persephone".

... καὶ ἀσμένας εἰς τὸν λειμῶνα ἀπιούσας οἶον ἐν πανηγύρει κατασκηνᾶσθαι,...

these souls subsequently happily advance towards the meadows [of Persephone] and they encamp there as people do when they go to a festival,...

First of all, we should clarify that, if the soul it directed to what corresponds to the inner Van Allen belt, then it has no reason to rejoice, because it seems that it gets reincarnated back on Earth quite soon.

At this point of the text, however, there is a very important piece of information about the path followed by our soul from the moment it will succeed to enter the "outer

Van Allen belt" after the death of its material body, which has to be presented.

Once again, this celebratory picture of an encampment described here is an encoded metaphor. In order to manage to understand the hidden meaning in detail, we should bring to our mind the view expressed by Plato in his *Symposium* pertaining to the existence of the "androgynous" species, through which he attempts to analyse the evolutionary path followed by our souls.

Thus, in the *Symposium* we are informed by Aristophanes that in the remote past there was a time when humans were "hermaphrodites", that is they had a body which was both male and female. These original (?) people were very powerful, however, posing a threat to gods, and thus Zeus at a certain evolutionary moment decided to bisect this androgynous species into male and female. Ever since that time, humans, possessing only the one of these separated parts, seek desperately for their other half.

The standard interpretations offered by modern scholars for that myth on the existence of two sexes, generally refer to the incarnated nature of humans; i.e. we adopt the explanation that from the bisection of the androgynous species originated the incarnated man and the incarnated woman. However, we should probably adopt another interpretation: that Plato does not refer to our material body, but rather to the path followed by our soul during its "fall" to Earth. Hence, these two "sexes" do not signify the incarnated men and women; instead, they are metaphors or code words for the masculine and the feminine part of the soul of every single incarnated human being.

We should know that for Plato our soul is not one-dimensional; instead, it consists of three parts, which compose the famous *trimereia*. These three parts are: The *epithymetikon*, the *thymetikon* or *thymoid*, and the *logistikon*.

The reason for the existence of the *trimereia* of our soul explains the fact that its three parts cannot evolve simultaneously, but instead they compulsorily follow a specific successive order.

According to this theory, the first part of the soul to acquire consciousness is the *logistikon*, followed by the two "mindless" parts, the *epithymetikon* and the *thymetikon*. According to the famous Chariot Allegory used by Plato in his dialogue *Phaedrus* (246a to 254e), our soul is like a chariot driven by a charioteer. The charioteer corresponds to the *logistikon* part of our soul. The chariot is pulled by two distinct winged horses; one of them is black and symbolizes the *epithymetikon* part of the soul, while the other horse is white and corresponds to its *thymoid* part.

In other words, the charioteer and the two horses represent the three parts of the human soul, while the chariot itself stands for the human body.

The reason our soul exists in this split state is that this way the charioteer can first evolve himself separately and then he will be able to better control the two mindless parts of the soul.

The *epithymetikon* part is the main self-conscious part of the soul; it is the one that gets reincarnated, the palpable and perceived part of our soul through our desires and appetites. This "black horse" operates only when we are awake.

The *thymoid* part is connected to the subconscious or unconscious; it lives in the "underworld" of Hades or in the meadows of Persephone and of course it is invisible and imperceptible. This "white horse" of our soul functions during our sleep.

Human as an entity appears similarly split into two parts:

I) The "inferior" self, which consists of the charioteer, the two horses and the chariot, and is described in Greek philosophy with the term *on* (Greek for "being").

II) The "superior" self, which resides in Hades and is described with the philosophical term *mi on*.

We observe that our inferior self is manifested during lifetime and wakefulness, while our superior self is manifested during when we are dead or when we sleep.

Throughout the life of a human, the one part (inferior self) seeks its other half, the other part (superior self), in order to be united with it and form once again an integrated and complete entity. This integrated entity is described with the philosophical term *ontos on*.

In other words, this points to us as a basic reason or destination, for which a human soul gets reincarnated, namely the evolution of its inferior self in order to be able to unite with the superior self. In such a case, the human would succeed in bringing into contact and operate together in a harmonious way the conscious and the unconscious part of the soul.

This development could be achieved only when the charioteer-mind, which belongs to the inferior self, acts, trying to find the way to control the two "horses" of opposite colours and qualities, the other parts of his inferior self.

Back to wordplay: The ancient Greek word for horse, *hippos*, has been replaced in modern Greek by the word *alogo*, which consists of the negation prefix (*a-*) and the neutral form of the word *logos* = reason, rational thinking. Similarly, the two *a-loga* parts of our soul do not have the capability to function on the basis of logic. Now, from the moment we acknowledge that these two parts of our soul are devoid of logic, we should also acknowledge that throughout our life they function antagonistically to one another and, as a consequence, they tend to pull the chariot towards opposite directions.

However, we should understand that this takes place only as long as our soul is enclosed inside its material body, which is symbolised with the chariot. From the moment of our body's death, our inferior self is "liberated" from the restraints of its material body and from that moment it can be united with its other half, which is its superior self that resides in Hades.

This is the meaning of the "encampment" mentioned in the ancient text of the *Republic*.

The "tent" our inferior self, free from the restraints of the material body, occupies and resides is essentially what the esoteric philosophy calls etheric body, in our context the body of the superior self, which, according to the views expressed by Plutarch in his essay "Face Which Appears in the Orb of the Moon" (Latin: *De facie in orbe lunae*), remains always in Hades or in the meadows of Persephone.

The notion of the holy "Festival", accordingly, alludes to the return of the formerly reincarnated part of the soul to the meadows of Persephone and to its encamping inside the tent of its superior self; the latter waits for the inferior self to welcome it with great joy.

This tent or shell of the superior self remains always unwearable and unchangeable in time, in an exact parallel with the relics of saints in the Catholic and Orthodox Christian tradition.

... καὶ ἀσπάζεσθαί τε ἀλλήλας ὅσαι γνώριμαι, ...

So the inferior self of each of these souls can be now united with its superior self (lit.: they greet each other), since is now able to recognise that self,...

These are the souls that have undergone some evolution during their incarnated life. It is interesting that a completely analogous procedure takes place here on Earth, in festivals of the Christian saints, during which the faithful kiss in veneration the relic of the saint honoured in the particular festival. In other words, a reason Christians are called to participate in the celebrations of a religious festival is to approach and kiss the holy relic of the saint, which corresponds to his or her superior self, the latter being able to keep the body intact after death, exactly as it happened in the case of Er!

This opportunity is then an event of unique value, because, although presumably it is impossible to come into contact with our own superior self as long as we live, Christians are offered the great opportunity to contact the superior self of a saint. The implicit aim here is to approach and embrace the way of life of that saint, just as we approach and kiss his or her material relic; this analogy corresponds in our Platonic context to the unification or the identification of our own superior self with the superior self of the saint. Probably Plato would appreciate the participation of Christians in the holy festivals of their saints, considering it as of paramount importance for the evolution of their souls! In ancient Greece, the holy festivals were taking place to honour the heroes, who essentially were venerated like the saints of the Orthodox and Catholic Christians.

In the ancient text there is the verb *aspazomai*, which in modern Greek took the meaning of "embracing and kissing", an interesting parallel with the shift of the Greek people from their ancient religion to Orthodox Christianity, in which the faithful kiss the relics of saints. However, in ancient Greek the meaning of the verb is "to greet as a friend, to hail, to be gladly accepted, to take care of, to strive for something for the love of it."[6]

All these functions represent the greeting that takes place between the inferior and the superior self. In other words, between our two selves is manifested a mutual and upgraded loving behaviour, a grand expression of the famous Platonic love, which characterises, as we have seen, the beloved habitat of our superior self.

Therefore, this is a very particular kind of greeting between our inferior and superior selves and Plato probably wants us to understand that this is the principal event that

6. Dimitrakos, D.: *Mega lexikon olis tis ellinikis glossis* (= Great Dictionary of All the Greek Language), N.Asimakopoulos & co., Athens 1964

takes place during the "holy festival" up there, and that whenever it takes place on Earth, it can be a representation of the greeting of our two selves in the "meadows of Persephone".[7]

... καὶ πυνθάνεσθαι τάς τε ἐκ τῆς γῆς ἤκουσας παρὰ τῶν ἑτέρων τὰ ἐκεῖ καὶ τὰς ἐκ τοῦ οὐρανοῦ τὰ παρ' ἐκείναις.

... and the two selves [united now in the tent] exchange information about their lives. The inferior self carries messages that concern his latest reincarnation on the Earth to his superior self,[8] while the superior self [being settled in the meadows of Persephone] transfers to the inferior self the remembrances from all the previous reincarnations [which will be needed for the selection of its new reincarnation].

This event of the communication between the two selves is extremely interesting, because it pertains to what is probably the most important process that has to do with the evolution of the human soul and can justify the reason of the human existence.

During this communication, a process of unique impor-

7. For a connection with the Pythagorean philosophy, see Charalampidis, George: *Pythagoras, o protos philosophos* (= Pythagoras, the First Philosopher), Oselotos publ., Athens 2013, p. 48
8. Charalampidis, George: *Aristotelous Peri mnimis kai anamniseos* (= Aristotle's *On Memory*), Oselotos publ., Athens 2011, p. 29. According to Aristotle, the self carries the "seals".

tance is achieved: Our inferior self, which has just "died", i.e. completed one more life in the cycle of his terrestrial reincarnations, must inform his superior self about the experiences he acquired through his last reincarnation. In other words, the inferior self has to transfer this temporary and perishable memory, which is stored in the brain cells of the material body, to the eternal and imperishable memory of the soul.

We should know that the function of memory is the prevailing issue concerning both the reason of our existence and the way our soul evolves.

Aristotle in his short treatise *Peri mnimis kai anamniseos* (Latin title: *De memoria et reminiscentia*, English title: *On Memory*) is especially revealing. He develops an entirely different theory from the one generally accepted nowadays, as he believes that an reincarnated person is equipped not only with his or her acquired mental memory, but also with an entirely different kind of memory, of opposite qualities.

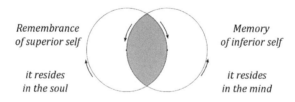

In addition to the acquired "memory of the brain", which pertains to our inferior self, each person unknowingly has an eternal "memory of the soul", which pertains to our superior self and is called *anamnisis* (remembrance) by Aristotle.

Hence, the memory of our brain is a temporary type of

memory, which humans use throughout their incarnated lives and lasts for as long as we are alive — parts of it most probably last for even less, as in the case of amnesia.

On the contrary, in the "white horse" part of the human soul resides the second, "secret" memory, the Aristotelian *anamnisis*, which is eternal because it resides in our superior self: in the Platonic metaphor, it is inside the tent. The *anamnisis* is destined to be transferred to the inferior self between two successive reincarnations.

We could compare the function of this memory of the soul to that of a large storage room, into which get always stored the memories of every successive reincarnation of the human soul. This procedure of "data transfer" takes place during the "holy festival" of the souls, following their singular "greeting".

We should understand that a main problem faced by every human is that these two memories are, by their very nature, mutually incompatible, at least as far as we are concerned. In other words, we do not know the manner through which we could bring them into any kind of mutual communication. For this reason, it is extremely difficult or impossible to recall during our reincarnated life the knowledge deposited in the eternal memory of our soul by its previous reincarnations.

This way of communication is indicated by Aristotle in his treatise *On Memory*. Plato himself seems to agree with these properties of the human soul and with the advanced Aristotelian theory on the subject, when he offers to us the mysterious phrase: "Knowledge is remembrance."[9]

As far as Pythagoras is concerned, he believes that the real Philosopher is the one who has the capability to organise for his students a proper "holy festival", so that during it the greeting of the two parts of the selves of his students can be achieved while they are alive; in this way, their remembrances could be transferred to their present lives.[10] Today, unfortunately, the "real Philosophers" of this kind have vanished altogether and, of course, the term "philosopher" has an entirely different meaning, while the retrieval of the remembrances of our souls from their previous reincarnations, if such a procedure exists, is an inconceivable dream.

Διηγεῖσθαι δὲ ἀλλήλαις τὰς μὲν ὀδυρομένας τε καὶ κλαούσας, ...

The two selves after their union communicate with each other, relating all the events that happened during the latest reincarnation on Earth, and they weep together, lamenting for the additional dreadful things they have been loaded with...

....

Here the weeping and lamenting in the plural number denotes that both the inferior and the superior self of the same person participate emotionally in this process of communication.

---

9. The theory of remembrance is examined by Plato in his dialogues *Meno, Phaedo, Phaedrus, Republic*, and *Symposium*.

10. Charalampidis, George: *Pythagoras, o protos philosophos*, Oselotos publ., Athens 2013, p. 48

The relation between the superior and the inferior self could be compared to the terrestrial life analogue of the relation between a teacher and his pupil. This association is presented in its perfect form through the dialectic method used by Socrates with his students.

In the parlance of Hinduism, Buddhism, Sikhism, and Jainism, this sum of the bad and good actions of a person on his or her terrestrial life are called karma.

... ἀναμιμνῃσκομένας ὅσα τε καὶ οἷα πάθοιεν καὶ ἴδοιεν ἐν τῇ ὑπὸ γῆς πορείᾳ – εἶναι δὲ τὴν πορείαν χιλιέτη

Because [through this greeting] the two selves are now in a position to remember again the number and the kind of misdeeds perpetrated by the inferior self during each reincarnation on Earth. And this cycle [of reincarnations of the inferior self] lasts a thousand years...

At this point there is another important information: Plato reveals to the reader that the human soul can never be reincarnated for only one life; from the moment it is decided that it will be reincarnated, it has to follow a cycle of reincarnations consisting of ten successive reincarnations.

– τὰς δ᾽ αὖ ἐκ τοῦ οὐρανοῦ εὐπαθείας διηγεῖσθαι καὶ θέας ἀμηχάνους τὸ κάλλος.

[Now if we examine the third case, of the absolutely vir-

tuous souls,] these proceed towards the higher heavenly fields, through the exterior sky. These souls, when they meet their superior self, they unite with it and transfer from the one self to the other the good events of their life; and then, as an integrated entity, they are able to view the divine beauty, to have visions of a beauty beyond words [or: because they have already acquired supernatural forces beyond words]

These are the souls destined to end up in the Isles of the Blessed, since they are so much evolved, and they have no reason to weep, as there is no misdeed that must be punished.

Τὰ μὲν οὖν πολλά, ὦ Γλαύκων, πολλοῦ χρόνου διηγήσασθαι.

However, the details [of the path of these perfected souls], my dear Glaucon, are so many that it would take too much time to tell it all.

It could be commented here that Socrates, in order to be able to know the many details that pertain to the functions of the perfected souls along their path towards the Isles of the Blessed, has his own soul belonging to this category of souls. In other words, Socrates, instead of following the path towards the Isles of the Blessed, chose with his own free will to return for one extra reincarnation to the Earth and play the role of the guide for humanity.

Chapter 4
THE SUM OF THE KARMA
OF OUR SOULS

Τὸ δ' οὖν κεφάλαιον ἔφη τόδε εἶναι, ὅσα πώποτέ τινα ἠδίκησαν καὶ ὅσους ἕκαστοι, ὑπὲρ ἁπάντων δίκην δεδωκέναι ἐν μέρει, ὑπὲρ ἑκάστου δεκάκις — τοῦτο δ' εἶναι κατὰ ἑκατονταετηρίδα [615b] ἑκάστην, ὡς βίου ὄντος τοσούτου τοῦ ἀνθρωπίνου — ἵνα δεκαπλάσιον τὸ ἔκτεισμα τοῦ ἀδικήματος ἐκτίνοιεν, καὶ οἷον εἴ τινες πολλοῖς θανάτων ἦσαν αἴτιοι, ἢ πόλεις προδόντες ἢ στρατόπεδα, καὶ εἰς δουλείας ἐμβεβληκότες ἤ τινος ἄλλης κακουχίας μεταίτιοι, πάντων τούτων δεκαπλασίας ἀλγηδόνας ὑπὲρ ἑκάστου κομίσαιντο, καὶ αὖ εἴ τινας εὐεργεσίας εὐεργετηκότες καὶ δίκαιοι καὶ ὅσιοι γεγονότες εἶεν, κατὰ ταὐτὰ [615c] τὴν ἀξίαν κομίζοιντο. τῶν δὲ εὐθὺς γενομένων καὶ ὀλίγον χρόνον βιούντων πέρι ἄλλα ἔλεγεν οὐκ ἄξια μνήμης. εἰς δὲ θεοὺς ἀσεβείας τε καὶ εὐσεβείας καὶ γονέας καὶ αὐτόχειρος φόνου μείζους ἔτι τοὺς μισθοὺς διηγεῖτο.

Τὸ δ' οὖν κεφάλαιον ἔφη τόδε εἶναι,...

[So now I will refer only to the words spoken by Er and pertain to] the way in which the sum of the debts is set

[which every soul has to pay off during its reincarnated life]...

We should understand that the "sum" mentioned in the ancient text is the set of the sins or the total indebtedness, in other words the "karma" of the soul, as we use to say nowadays, influenced by the Hinduistic term. This is regarded as the reason for the reincarnation of a soul.

In this view, our soul carries into each life it is reincarnated a certain amount of debt, and should work hard in order to manage to earn the required "money" that will allow this soul to pay it off within the length of its terrestrial life. By paying off this debt, the soul will achieve a cleansing, which will open the road for that soul's evolution, until the final unification with the superior self.

The work we must do in order to pay off our debt pertains to the better understanding and application of the virtue that will lead us to achieve a virtuous way of life. This work must begin from the study of philosophy, through which a person is able to cleanse his or her soul from its various passions, while in parallel this person must pursue the evolution of his or her soul.

... ὅσα πώποτέ τινα ἠδίκησαν...

[This sum was accumulated] because of all the wrongs these souls had ever done to anyone during all their previous lives...

... καὶ ὅσους ἕκαστοι,...

... and because of the number of all people whom they had separately wronged,...

It is extremely interesting that at this point Plato explains to us the manner through which our soul has been indebted with this karmic sum that now has to pay off. He describes that the sum from which we must be cleansed has been accumulated upon our soul by two different sources:

A. The total number of wrongdoings we have committed.

B. The total number of persons whom we have wronged in any way.

... ὑπὲρ ἁπάντων δίκην δεδωκέναι ἐν μέρει,...

The sum of these debts is not recorded only through the judgement of merely one life,...

... ὑπὲρ ἑκάστου δεκάκις...

... but it is accumulated as the recordings of many judgements [actually the sum of the judgements of the wrong actions of the given soul during all its previous reincarnations] and the corresponding penalties are defined accordingly: for each one of these, the soul is punished to be reincarnated ten times...

This is the thousand-year cycle of the soul, which Plato

mentioned earlier and the function of which remains completely unknown. This is still another point of extreme interest, since it reveals to us that our soul is reincarnated with the prospect of its cleansing, which can be completed only after at least ten lives and by no means during only one life, as one could believe.

In other words, a single condemnation of the soul corresponds to a cycle of ten reincarnations, which has a length of the order of a thousand years, in order to succeed to complete the paying off of its debts. And hence, the definitive decision of the judges concerning the path of the soul in the future takes place after the end of the tenth reincarnation.

If this is so, then one of the basic and indispensable pieces of metaphysical knowledge every person should know is the function of this *post mortem* "judgement mechanism", which, however, remains totally unknown. If people could ever have a positive knowledge of such a karmic judgement, many would probably decide that they must exploit in the best possible way the entire time period of the thousand years in order to fix their wrongdoings.

Aristotle seems to support this theory of the ten reincarnations: he suggests that, to the end of its integration, the soul has to remember and realise, through meditation, the wrongs perpetrated during the nine previous reincarnations, so that these wrongs can be fixed and the soul can achieve purification.[11]

In other words, according to Plato, we should realise that

---

11. Charalampidis, George: *Pythagoras, o protos philosophos*, Oselotos publ., Athens 2013

until our tenth life we have the opportunity to remember and to mend in time all the wrongs and mistakes we have perpetrated during our nine previous reincarnations, up to the present day.

Otherwise, we will continue to repeat the same wrong-doings during our next reincarnations, so we will return on Earth mandatorily, to start a subsequent cycle of another ten reincarnations, with the aim to start from the beginning a new effort towards our perfection, as the previous time we obviously failed.

— τοῦτο δ᾽ εἶναι κατὰ ἑκατονταετηρίδα [615b] ἑκά-στην, ὡς βίου ὄντος τοσούτου τοῦ ἀνθρωπίνου —...

... — and this [i.e. the previous reference to millennia] is because a human life lasts for about a hundred years each, if we calculate the average duration of a life cycle from one reincarnation to the next —...

That is, we get reincarnated on Earth in order to complete 10 life cycles of 100 years each on the average, so that we will complete the thousand years of the compulsory cycle of "erasing" the debts of our soul.

Of course, this means that only once per ten centuries, after the completion of these ten reincarnations, we are subjected to the definite judgement by the judges of Hades, and during this large time period we must have paid back the entire sum of the debts of our soul. If, despite this huge amount of time, we fail, then new cycles of reincarnations are in store for us.

... ἵνα δεκαπλάσιον τὸ ἔκτεισμα τοῦ ἀδικήματος ἐκτίνοιεν,...

... because each soul will have to be subjected to a punishment equal to ten times the crime...

So Plato reveals to us the "price list" of the punishments a given soul must undergo in order to be acquitted from its debts!

This passage can be taken to mean that the cost of each single crime is ten reincarnations! In order to better understand the way such a universal justice functions according to the philosopher, we can offer certain examples:

If we wrong one person during our current reincarnation, then our soul will be charged with ten future reincarnations within the next 1,000 years in order to pay back for this unjust act.

If we wrong two persons during the same reincarnation, then our soul will be charged with twenty future reincarnations within the next 2,000 years in order to pay back for these two unjust acts.

If we wrong three persons by perpetrating two wrongdoings against *each one* of them, then our soul will be charged with sixty future reincarnations, which will last for 6,000 years.

Finally, if we wrong during each one of the ten lives of an reincarnation cycle one person at a time, then our soul will be charged with one hundred future reincarnations, which will last for ten millennia. And so on.

According to this scheme, we have to admit that we should not be puzzled about the reason we are still here on Earth, trapped inside endless cycles of reincarnations, trying to understand what kind of mistakes we have done in our previous reincarnations and for what reason we are being punished.

... καὶ οἶον εἴ τινες πολλοῖς θανάτων ἦσαν αἴτιοι,...

... and there is also the case that certain persons have been the cause of many human deaths,...

... ἢ πόλεις προδόντες ἢ στρατόπεδα, καὶ εἰς δουλείας ἐμβεβληκότες ἤ τινος ἄλλης κακουχίας μεταίτιοι,...

... or they have betrayed the population of a city or an army, and hence they have led to that army's enslavement, or have participated in any other iniquity against a whole population;...

... πάντων τούτων δεκαπλασίας ἀλγηδόνας ὑπὲρ ἑκά-στου κομίσαιντο,...

... then all the souls of these wrongdoers might receive in requital punishments tenfold for each of these wrongs.

....

This line can also be taken to mean that the duration of

101

the punishments will span ten lives of 100 years (on the average) for each person they have harmed. In such a case, let us see another example: If a city has a population of 20,000 and a political leader of that city applies an unjust law, which has a negative net effect for all 20,000 citizens, then this politician should receive a punishment that will force him or her to reincarnate 200,000 (two hundred thousand) times in the future; and these reincarnations will last for 20,000,000 (twenty million) years!

We see that in such a case of a "group injustice" the sum of the karma of a soul increases rather suddenly to preposterous levels, since for each harmed person separately and for each individual harm caused to every person, a thousand years of requital are needed.

It is very important to know whether Plato suggests this way of function of the "punishment mechanism" for the souls, and, conversely, of the "reward mechanism". As we will see in the following, the great philosopher believes this is the only way we will achieve someday to pay back our moral debts, since the notion of the universal justice pertains to the total progress of our souls.

... καὶ αὖ εἴ τινας εὐεργεσίας εὐεργετηκότες καὶ δί-καιοι καὶ ὅσιοι γεγονότες εἶεν, κατὰ ταῦτὰ τὴν ἀξίαν κομίζοιντο.

On the other side, if someone has done deeds of kindness and been just and holy throughout his [or her] life, in the same way one could estimate his [or her] due reward.

Here we are informed that the sum of the karma is an "algebraic sum", in the sense that it contains both negative and positive values, which are subtracted or added, respectively. If the same measure is used for both, then in principle for every good deed we accomplish during our life, and for every person in need we help, a thousand years of punishment are removed from the total debt of our soul. In this point, therefore, we are presented the way we could be relieved from the punishments of thousands of years, which our soul is supposed to be forced to suffer through successive reincarnations. In Christian terminology, we are given the way we could be absolved from the sinful acts our soul has committed in the past, even because of ignorance.

Our conscious study of philosophy, to the extent it can lead us to understand our mistakes and to upgrade our behaviour, could, in principle, assist in reversing a negative "algebraic sum".

The specific Platonic myth we are dealing with, since it has to do with the soul of Er, who is from Armenia, could be compared to the myth of Prometheus, who is chained to the Caucasus, just to the north of Armenia; likewise, a human soul is bound to a long series of reincarnations, from which the soul of Er has managed to escape.

Undoubtedly, this "Law of Good Acts" is a hope-giving message Plato wants to offer to his readers, indirectly prompting them to apply it in order to find the solution for the salvation of their souls and the annulment of their debts. The great secret that could liberate the souls of the readers from the almost endless punishments inflicted upon them because of their repeated and continuing mistakes, is to consciously do as many good acts we can and to help as many persons as possible. This is the only path to the salvation of our souls.

As a well-known modern Greek proverbial phrase goes, "Do the Good and throw it to the sea": This means that, in case we perform a good act by helping a person, we should not expect or wait to receive directly a reward from that person. This "expected" reward will be administered to us, according to Plato, by the judges of Hades, when they will judge our soul, by reducing our number of reincarnations. A corollary of this is that the value of good actions cannot be calculated by us, however it is the only solution we have to understand, accept and adopt at any cost.

Τῶν δὲ εὐθὺς γενομένων καὶ ὀλίγον χρόνον βιούντων πέρι ἄλλα ἔλεγεν οὐκ ἄξια μνήμης.

And for those who had just been born, as well as for those who have lived for a very short time on Earth, he (Er) said that other processes are followed, not worthy to be recorded by our minds at this point.

....

What Plato wants to convey here is that there are also special cases, each of which has its own value. However, it would be meaningless to refer to these particular cases at this moment; because what must occupy us is the understanding of the situation in which an ordinary reincarnated soul is found.

Εἰς δὲ θεοὺς ἀσεβείας τε καὶ εὐσεβείας ...

While for those who have shown piety or impiety towards the gods,...

... καὶ γονέας καὶ αὐτόχειρος φόνου μείζους ἔτι τοὺς μισθοὺς διηγεῖτο.

... and for those who have murdered either their own parents or themselves, he had even greater requitals to tell.

In other words, persons who respect the gods, their parents and themselves, can through their piety subtract more than a thousand years of punishment from the karma of their souls.

A modern reader could probably be impressed by the extreme importance placed by Plato on the issue of respect towards gods, our parents and, concurrently, towards our own self. The philosopher assigns to a similar category the cases of suicide and parricide (the killing of a parent); moreover, he considers both these acts to be almost equivalent to impiety towards the gods! Of great importance, hence, is to avoid hurting not only other persons, but also our own self, as for example through abuses, or by any other possible means.

Chapter 5
THE CASE OF ARDIAEUS THE TYRANT

Ἔφη γὰρ δὴ παραγενέσθαι ἐρωτωμένῳ ἑτέρῳ ὑπὸ ἑτέρου ὅπου εἴη Ἀρδιαῖος ὁ μέγας. ὁ δὲ Ἀρδιαῖος οὗτος τῆς Παμφυλίας ἔν τινι πόλει τύραννος ἐγεγόνει, ἤδη χιλιοστὸν ἔτος εἰς ἐκεῖνον τὸν χρόνον, γέροντά τε πατέρα ἀποκτείνας [615d] καὶ πρεσβύτερον ἀδελφόν, καὶ ἄλλα δὴ πολλά τε καὶ ἀνόσια εἰργασμένος, ὡς ἐλέγετο. ἔφη οὖν τὸν ἐρωτώμενον εἰπεῖν, «οὐχ ἥκει,» φάναι, «οὐδ' ἂν ἥξει δεῦρο. ἐθεασάμεθα γὰρ οὖν δὴ καὶ τοῦτο τῶν δεινῶν θεαμάτων· ἐπειδὴ ἐγγὺς τοῦ στομίου ἦμεν μέλλοντες ἀνιέναι καὶ τἆλλα πάντα πεπονθότες, ἐκεῖνόν τε κατείδομεν ἐξαίφνης καὶ ἄλλους-σχεδόν τι αὐτῶν τοὺς πλείστους τυράννους· ἦσαν δὲ καὶ ἰδιῶταί τινες τῶν [615e] μεγάλα ἡμαρτηκότων-οὓς οἰομένους ἤδη ἀναβήσεσθαι οὐκ ἐδέχετο τὸ στόμιον, ἀλλ' ἐμυκᾶτο ὁπότε τις τῶν οὕτως ἀνιάτως ἐχόντων εἰς πονηρίαν ἢ μὴ ἱκανῶς δεδωκὼς δίκην ἐπιχειροῖ ἀνιέναι. ἐνταῦθα δὴ ἄνδρες, ἔφη, ἄγριοι, διάπυροι ἰδεῖν, παρεστῶτες καὶ καταμανθάνοντες τὸ φθέγμα, τοὺς μὲν διαλαβόντες ἦγον, τὸν δὲ Ἀρδιαῖον καὶ ἄλλους συμποδίσαντες [616a] χεῖράς τε καὶ πόδας καὶ κεφαλήν, καταβαλόντες καὶ ἐκδείραντες, εἷλκον παρὰ τὴν ὁδὸν ἐκτὸς ἐπ' ἀσπαλάθων κνάμπτοντες, καὶ τοῖς ἀεὶ παριοῦσι σημαίνοντες ὧν ἕνεκά τε καὶ ὅτι εἰς τὸν Τάρταρον ἐμπεσούμενοι ἄγοιντο.»

ἔνθα δὴ φόβων, ἔφη, πολλῶν καὶ παντοδαπῶν σφίσι γεγονότων, τοῦτον ὑπερβάλλειν, μὴ γένοιτο ἑκάστῳ τὸ φθέγμα ὅτε ἀναβαίνοι, καὶ ἀσμενέστατα ἕκαστον σιγήσαντος ἀναβῆναι. καὶ τὰς μὲν δὴ δίκας τε καὶ τιμωρίας τοιαύτας τινὰς [616b] εἶναι, καὶ αὖ τὰς εὐεργεσίας ταύταις ἀντιστρόφους.

Ἔφη γὰρ δὴ παραγενέσθαι ἐρωτωμένῳ ἑτέρῳ ὑπὸ ἑτέρου ὅπου εἴη Ἀρδιαῖος ὁ μέγας.

[After these revelations about the punishments and the rewards of the souls] Er said that he stood by when one [soul] was questioned by another "Where could Ardiaeus the Great be?"

Ὁ δὲ Ἀρδιαῖος οὗτος τῆς Παμφυλίας ἔν τινι πόλει τύραννος ἐγεγόνει, ἤδη χιλιοστὸν ἔτος εἰς ἐκεῖνον τὸν χρόνον,...

This Ardiaeus had been tyrant in a certain city of Pamphylia just a thousand years before that time,...

....

In the vein of those said about the reincarnation cycle, it could be argued that the soul of Ardiaeus was at that time completing its tenth life in the cycle of the thousand years of reincarnations.

We should understand, of course, that the person of Ardiaeus as a Pamphylian tyrant symbolically represents all those in power, irrespectively of the race to which they belong, from the moment the way they govern and the laws they impose do not enlighten the souls of their subjects or citizens, but instead they harm them.

According to the revelations of the previous chapter, we should assume that Ardiaeus had no other chance of purification, as he was at the end of his tenth reincarnation, i.e. at the point at which the time had come for his soul to be judged irrevocably and, accordingly, the future path for this soul to be decided.

... γέροντά τε πατέρα ἀποκτείνας καὶ πρεσβύτερον ἀδελφόν, καὶ ἄλλα δὴ πολλά τε καὶ ἀνόσια εἰργασμένος, ὡς ἐλέγετο.

... and it was widely known that he had put to death his aged father and his elder brother, and that he also had done many other unholy deeds.

Ἔφη οὖν τὸν ἐρωτώμενον εἰπεῖν,...

So Er said that the one questioned replied,...

... «οὐχ ἥκει», φάναι, «οὐδ᾽ ἂν ἥξει δεῦρο.

... "he has not come", said he, "nor will he be likely to come here".

When the souls are in Hades, Plato assumes that they have a full knowledge and understanding of the mistakes they and other souls have made, but now it is too late for them. If Ardiaeus had this awareness as long as he lived on

Earth, he certainly would have avoided committing such serious crimes at any cost.

However, this is exactly the purpose of philosophy, which according to Plato is the most eminent "study of death".[12] What the great philosopher suggests is that through philosophy we could realise the accumulated mistakes made by our soul before we die. In such a case, we would normally have in our disposal the required amount of time to compensate for our misdeeds; thus, we would not have their burden in the sum of our debt, which would be relieved as much as possible with the accomplishment of many good acts.

Therefore, we should be especially careful and should have the full awareness of our actions, so that we will never reach the point when it will be said for us what was said for the soul of Ardiaeus: "he has not come, nor will he be likely to come here". The soul of the tyrant would never be given another chance for salvation. Being in Hades, that soul realised how serious were the crimes perpetrated during the reincarnated life of Ardiaeus, and that the years of punishment in the form of future reincarnations would be endless. Thus, the soul realised that, in practice, there was no possibility to be cleansed from these crimes for eons to come!

Ἐθεασάμεθα γὰρ οὖν δὴ καὶ τοῦτο τῶν δεινῶν θεαμάτων:...

---

12. *Phaedo,* 63b4 – 69e2

*"For this example of Ardiaeus was indeed one of the
dreadful sights we beheld [we thus learned that there
is an additional case of soul punishment, which is the
most tragic];*

This most tragic case for the evolutionary path of the human soul is to be deprived of the right to be reincarnated again. This happens because it is virtually impossible to pay back the tremendous sum of the debt that this soul has accumulated because of its crimes.

Ἐπειδὴ ἐγγὺς τοῦ στομίου ἦμεν μέλλοντες ἀνιέναι
καὶ τἆλλα πάντα πεπονθότες,...

*When we were [as a group of souls] near the entrance
of a void, from where we would ascend, as the process of
our judgement had been ended,...*

...ἐκεῖνόν τε κατείδομεν ἐξαίφνης καὶ ἄλλους,...

*... we suddenly caught sight of Ardiaeus [who also had
been judged] and of a group of other souls,...*

... — σχεδόν τι αὐτῶν τοὺς πλείστους τυράννους:

— the most of them being souls of tyrants;

Here we can assume that after the end of their judgement the souls form groups according to their quality.

ἦσαν δὲ καὶ ἰδιῶταί τινες τῶν μεγάλα ἡμαρτηκότων —...

but also along with them were some private citizens, of those who had committed great crimes —...

... οὓς οἰομένους ἤδη ἀναβήσεσθαι οὐκ ἐδέχετο τὸ στόμιον,...

... and when these [sinful souls] supposed that at last they were about to ascend, the opening of the void itself would not allow them to enter,...

... ἀλλ' ἐμυκᾶτο ὁπότε τις τῶν οὕτως ἀνιάτως ἐχόντων εἰς πονηρίαν ἢ μὴ ἱκανῶς δεδωκὼς δίκην ἐπιχειροῖ ἀνιέναι».

... but it bellowed in a threatening way whenever anyone of these wicked souls, whose wickedness remained incurable up to that moment, or of those who had not adequately completed the procedure of their judgement, attempted to come up the opening."

In other words, we conclude that in the region where the judgement was taking place, in addition to the physical presence of the judges themselves, something that today we would call technological measures was taken: There was a highly advanced "detector of wicked souls", which automatically prevented the entrance of such souls to the region destined for the higher evolutionary stages. A modern reader might compare this process to the metal detectors in the gates of entrance to the departure rooms of the airports.

«Ἐνταῦθα δὴ ἄνδρες», ἔφη, «ἄγριοι, διάπυροι ἰδεῖν,...

"And thereupon", Er said, "there were also savage humanoid figures of fiery aspect...

... παρεστῶτες καὶ καταμανθάνοντες τὸ φθέγμα,...

... standing by and taking note of the judgement that had been issued about each soul;,...

... τοὺς μὲν διαλαβόντες ἦγον,...

... these figures were arresting the souls of the private citizens, taking them away,...

... τὸν δὲ Ἀρδιαῖον καὶ ἄλλους συμποδίσαντες χεῖράς τε καὶ πόδας καὶ κεφαλήν, καταβαλόντες καὶ ἐκδείραντες,...

... but they bound Ardiaeus and the other tyrants [who had committed similar crimes] hand and foot and head, and threw them down and flayed them,...

Obviously, from this point begins the procedure of punishment of the most guilty souls. When a certain soul ends up being so unjust that has no more the ability of cleansing, as a result it must be flayed.

But what does this mean? Since all souls are immaterial, the only adequate interpretation of this "flaying" procedure is, we believe, the irrevocable and definite erasure of all the recordings of their memory. This can be aptly compared to a vinyl phonograph record that gets scratched; afterwards, it cannot reproduce the music that had been recorded on its surface, and therefore it is useless. In other words, if the soul gets completely "scratched" and cannot come into contact with its remembrances, then it is destined to be thrown as a piece of garbage, much like a scratched vinyl record.

... εἷλκον παρὰ τὴν ὁδὸν ἐκτὸς ἐπ' ἀσπαλάθων κνάμπτοντες,...

... and they also dragged them by the wayside [out of all three roads of the trivium of the Persephone meadows], carding them on thorns,...

Here we can observe that probably any soul that in any way deviates out of the designated paths, which may be compared to energetic fields (the "meadows of Persephone"), feels like being scratched by thorns. It is essentially the continuation of the "flaying", until the content of all the recordings in the memories of the criminal souls are erased forever and destroyed completely.

... καὶ τοῖς ἀεὶ παριοῦσι σημαίνοντες ὧν ἕνεκά τε καὶ ὅτι εἰς τὸν Τάρταρον ἐμπεσούμενοι ἄγοιντο.»

... announcing to those souls who are always present in such a judgement process for what cause [the soul of Ardiaeus and the other souls of his group] were carried away, and that they will throw them down to the main core of Tartarus".

The reason it is announced to the souls who are always present in the "Van Allen belts" that the soul of Ardiaeus will end up falling into the Tartarus, is the need to set this process as an example of what to avoid, so that all these souls would take care during their next reincarnation not to act like Ardiaeus, for if they do, they must know that they will have the same end.

Now we are in a position to understand that the "flaying" of the soul is a metaphor for the destruction or deletion of its entire evolutionary history/path, which was stored in its memory, because that would be the only way to be separated from its mistakes, from the moment it was judged as unreceptive of learning.

So this throwing of the soul into Tartarus is the worst case scenario for the evolutionary path a given soul can take, as in such a case the soul loses all the memories and experiences gathered from all previous reincarnations.

We could suppose that in such a case this soul is forced to start from the beginning its activity. In the Hindu tradition, this means that it would have to start from being embodied in a stone, then it would be "promoted" to a plant, subsequently to an animal and eventually it would be reincarnated into a human body, if it had enough time; because the time lost for a soul that falls into the Tartarus can be compared to eternity, and the evolutionary distance that separates the condemned soul from the others is immense.

―――――――――――――――――――――――――――

«Ἔνθα δὴ φόβων», ἔφη, «πολλῶν καὶ παντοδαπῶν σφίσι γεγονότων, τοῦτον ὑπερβάλλειν,...

As Er said, although many and various processes and events had been experienced by them [in the time period just before, during and after their judgement], this fear exceeded all...:

... μὴ γένοιτο ἑκάστῳ τὸ φθέγμα ὅτε ἀναβαίνοι,...

... that of the bellowing of the entrance [to the outer belt], lest each one should hear the voice when he tried to go up...

....

Evidently, if the souls do not hear the bellowing of the gate, they will be able to ascend to the "outer Van Allen belt"; and this event offers them the opportunity to advance in their evolutionary process, all the more because in such a case they will be given the possibility to select their next reincarnation.

... καὶ ἀσμενέστατα ἕκαστον σιγήσαντος ἀναβῆναι.»

... *and each went up most gladly when the entrance had kept silence; that was the greatest expectance of every soul."*

It would be reasonable to conclude from this phrase that the entrance to the "outer Van Allen belt" (where only the just souls had the right to ascend) would bellow all too often, since obviously the majority of the souls that attempted to pass through it would not be righteous. This is the reason that the greatest hope of a given soul was to avoid hearing its bellowing when it would enter it.

Καὶ τὰς μὲν δὴ δίκας τε καὶ τιμωρίας τοιαύτας τινὰς εἶναι,...

And the judgements and penalties were somewhat after this manner [for the souls acknowledge that, if they have made grave mistakes, it would be fair to be punished heavily for them],...

... καὶ αὖ τὰς εὐεργεσίας ταύταις ἀντιστρόφους.

... while if, on the contrary, they were good souls, they are worthy of any blessing.

117

As a final conclusion, it should by now be absolutely clear that the souls which are reincarnated on planet Earth are here in order to serve their penalty because of specific misdeeds they have committed during previous reincarnations, and not in order to "have a nice time". This view of the Earth as a place of sorrow reminds us of the Platonic view of the body as a prison for the soul, which passed to several Fathers of the Christian Church.

It is quite important to have in mind this view, because according to it the human soul should always be focused on how it will manage to correct its old mistakes, in addition to being very careful in order not to fall into new mistakes, which will increase its burden even more.

In this evolutionary process of the soul, according to Plato, its only true allies are the teachings of ancient Greek philosophy.

The integrated orbits of the planets Earth and Venus produce this wonderful figure, which represents their relative motions during a long period of time.

Chapter 6
A PLATONIC DESCRIPTION OF THE UNIVERSE

Ἐπειδὴ δὲ τοῖς ἐν τῷ λειμῶνι ἑκάστοις ἑπτὰ ἡμέραι γένοιντο, ἀναστάντας ἐντεῦθεν δεῖν τῇ ὀγδόῃ πορεύεσθαι, καὶ ἀφικνεῖσθαι τεταρταίους ὅθεν καθορᾶν ἄνωθεν διὰ παντὸς τοῦ οὐρανοῦ καὶ γῆς τεταμένον φῶς εὐθύ, οἷον κίονα, μάλιστα τῇ ἴριδι προσφερῆ, λαμπρότερον δὲ καὶ καθαρώτερον· εἰς ὃ ἀφικέσθαι προελθόντες ἡμερησίαν ὁδόν, καὶ ἰδεῖν αὐτόθι κατὰ [616c] μέσον τὸ φῶς ἐκ τοῦ οὐρανοῦ τὰ ἄκρα αὐτοῦ τῶν δεσμῶν τεταμένα-εἶναι γὰρ τοῦτο τὸ φῶς σύνδεσμον τοῦ οὐρανοῦ, οἷον τὰ ὑποζώματα τῶν τριήρων, οὕτω πᾶσαν συνέχον τὴν περιφοράν.

Ἐπειδὴ δὲ τοῖς ἐν τῷ λειμῶνι ἑκάστοις ἑπτὰ ἡμέραι γένοιντο,...

Some of the souls who [pass through the entrance and] ascend to the meadows of Persephone, remain there for seven days...

... ἀναστάντας ἐντεῦθεν δεῖν τῇ ὀγδόῃ πορεύεσθαι, καὶ ἀφικνεῖσθαι τεταρταίους...

... and then they rise up on the eighth day and journey on [leaving the meadows]; they are led to another region, which they reach four days later.

... ὅθεν καθορᾶν ἄνωθεν διὰ παντὸς τοῦ οὐρανοῦ καὶ γῆς τεταμένον φῶς εὐθύ,...

From this [unknown] region, [these privileged souls] can clearly discern a light extending in a straight line from above, throughout the heaven and the [orbit of the] Earth,...

Plato now goes on to describe for the first time an unknown region in the sky, which has some quite properties we should examine.

From this region, instead of beholding the light of the Sun in the form of a disc, as we see it from the Earth, the souls discern a light in the form of a straight luminous line, which can be compared to observing the Sun in an added time-lapse sequence, showing a part of its trajectory through the Galaxy (small parts of this trajectory are almost straight lines). We should know that this luminous line, as an added time-lapse sequence, can also represent what in modern physics is called the "arrow of time", the visualisation of the fourth dimension of spacetime.

Extending this metaphor, it could be argued that these privileged souls, who were favourably judged, acquire capabilities we would consider impossible, such as the power to observe regions of spacetime, i.e. different moments of time simultaneously!

Alternatively, we could ask: Is there a region in space from where one could observe the motion of the Sun and its planets as a whole? In order to be able to identify a celestial place with such a singular property, we must have the adequate special astronomical knowledge, in other words we must have covered the "scientific gap" in order to understand the full range of metaphors and interpretations this ancient text can offer.

Where, then, can such a celestial region exist?

Undoubtedly, it should be very far from the Earth; given the great distance the souls have to travel until they reach it, which is alluded to in the text when it mentions the "four-day" travel required, we could place it in the remote region of our planetary system that is known as the Kuiper Belt (or, more appropriately, the Edgeworth-Kuiper Belt).

Hence, in addition to the Van Allen radiation belts, we can name another host for the souls after the death of their material bodies: the Kuiper Belt welcomes the absolutely righteous souls in order to offer them both the proper residing conditions they now deserve and the opportunities to experience and understand other perspectives and higher dimensions of the Universe, something that is impossible for any human during his or her bodily life on Earth.

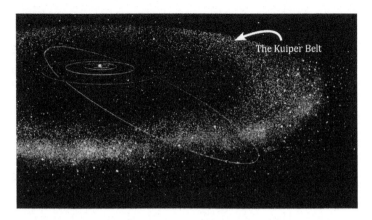

The Kuiper Belt is an outer disc or wide ring of small icy bodies that revolve around the Sun beyond the planets of the Solar System.

Since the Edgeworth-Kuiper Belt is a circumstellar disc of many small bodies that revolve extremely slowly around the Sun beyond all the planets of the Solar System, it is evidently a place that, while still a part of the Solar System, offers a unique vantage point for the combined observation of the motions of both the Sun and all its planets.

We should stress the fact that the existence of this belt was suggested for the first time only in the twentieth century, first by the Irish astronomer and economist Kenneth E. Edgeworth (1880-1972), and ten years later, in 1951, by the great Dutch-American planetary astronomer Gerard P. Kuiper (1905-1973). And that the first observational evidence for its existence came only as recently as in August 1992 with the discovery of the first Kuiper belt object (KBO), although the dwarf planet Pluto, which was discovered in 1930, is now also considered to be a KBO.

The main suspicion for the existence of the Edgeworth-Kuiper Belt came from the study of the orbits of short-period comets around the Sun, which indicated that they must originate from such a disc-shaped region. Nowadays, after the discovery of many KBOs, it is known that this belt consists of a large number of minor planets of the outer Solar System. It has the shape of a thick disc and extends from a distance of 30 AU to about 50 AU from the Sun (1 AU, or astronomical unit, is the average Earth-Sun distance, 149.6 million km). It contains a few dwarf planets, such as Pluto, Haumea, and Makemake, and hundreds of thousands of cometary nuclei, i.e. bodies that when are perturbed enough to "fall" in the inner Solar System they develop a coma and tail, becoming comets.

The Edgeworth-Kuiper Belt can be regarded as a second asteroid belt in our Solar System, beyond the Main asteroid belt, which extends between the orbits of Mars and Jupiter.

... οἶον κίονα, μάλιστα τῇ ἴριδι προσφερῆ, λαμπρότερον δὲ καὶ καθαρώτερον...

... and this luminous set resembles in its shape a column of a temple and shows around it the seven colours of the rainbow, but in a much brighter and clearer form.

We should note that all humans on Earth can perceive only the three dimensions of space and time as a clearly distinct dimensional entity, the so-called "arrow of time". Moreover, this temporal dimension can be perceived in the three-dimensional world we live in only as a set of points.

This means that we cannot perceive the trajectories followed by the celestial bodies, although all of them move, even at very high speeds; instead, we observe them only at certain points of their trajectories, which change their positions in the sky as time passes.

If, however, we observed from somewhere inside the Kuiper Belt, in other words at a very large distance from the Sun, and could perceive the time as just a fourth dimension, visualising the motion of the celestial bodies during a considerable time span, then we would have probably compared our planetary system to a four-dimensional column. Such a column, which could move in time, would be described by a mathematician as a "hyper-column".

This is the exact analogy of what the souls of the dead behold, according to Plato, when they arrive in that remote region. This points to the fact that the evolution of the souls has to do also with their ability to understand the higher dimensions, something that human beings are absolutely incapable of.

We know that the motions of the planets around the Sun, if they could be observed in the fourth dimension, would be seen as orbits that would trace in the circumference of the column described above a series of grooves. The central axis of the column would correspond to the Sun.

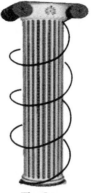

| The Sun | The Sun |
| as a point in time | as a "hyper-column" |

This bright column with its grooves could be visualised as the trace of many luminous objects in the depth of time, as it can be reproduced by a modern computer.

In other words, this column, which as observed in the four dimensions is called a hyper-column, would represent the path of the Sun through time, and it would have all the planets tracing helixes around it, which most simply could be recognized from one another with the aid of their colours, in a clearer form than the slightly blurred colours of a rainbow.

... εἰς ὃ ἀφικέσθαι προελθόντες ἡμερησίαν ὁδόν,...

... To this new region they [these privileged souls] arrive after they have followed an itinerary, throughout which

they are illuminated by daylight.

. . . .

We notice that during the four-day journey of these special souls they follow a route during which there is always daylight, in other words the light of the Sun, and no night at all.

It is evident that this sunlit path could be a metaphor of a trajectory in a direction towards the Kuiper belt. All these souls have to follow the same route.

We know that the average distance of the Kuiper belt from the Sun and from the Earth is about 40 astronomical units (AU); thus, we could very easily calculate in this metaphor the average speed these souls would travel at, through ordinary space, since they need 4 days to reach the belt: the souls would move with the tremendous speed of 10 AU per day, or 62.3 million kilometres per hour (39 million m.p.h.). This corresponds to about 5.8 percent of the speed of light. Remember that 1 AU is the average distance between the Earth and the Sun; so such a soul, travelling at the same speed, could within a single day travel from the Earth to the Sun and back 5 times!

... καὶ ἰδεῖν αὐτόθι κατὰ μέσον τὸ φῶς ἐκ τοῦ οὐρανοῦ τὰ ἄκρα αὐτοῦ τῶν δεσμῶν τεταμένα,...

[These particular souls] are able to see from that region at the middle of the light the edges of its fastenings stretched from heaven...

... – εἶναι γὰρ τοῦτο τὸ φῶς σύνδεσμον τοῦ οὐρανοῦ, οἷον τὰ ὑποζώματα τῶν τριήρων,...

... because this light was the girdle of the heavens like the undergirders of triremes,...

The "middle of the light" corresponds in our metaphor to the light of the hyper-column that passes from the middle (centre) of the circle formed by the Kuiper belt, that is from the position of the Sun; and from the edges of the solar hyper-column, the souls could see all the planets attached (fastened) to it, by the invisible bonds of gravity. Also, the planets are connected to each other by the same kind of bonds.

Now the light of the hyper-column can be taken to represent the combined light of all the planets and the Sun together ("girdle"). The hyper-column with the grooves of the planetary orbits upon it resembled the "undergirders", i.e. the internal stretched cables (about 47 mm thick) that held together the hull of the triremes, or possibly the internal ladders that probably connected the three levels (rows) of the triremes. The description of the ancient text allows for the "ladder" interpretation, however the existence of such ladders, although rational, is not mentioned in any other ancient source.

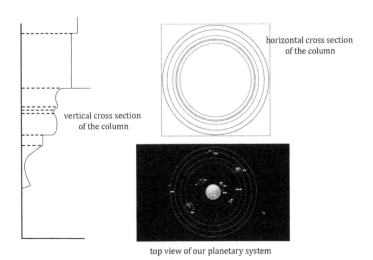

top view of our planetary system

The top view of our planetary system is very similar to the cross-sectional view of a column of an ancient Greek temple. With the time dimension added, it produces a hyper-column of four dimensions.

... οὕτω πᾶσαν συνέχον τὴν περιφοράν.

... which hold together in a similar way the entire revolving system.

This is the view presented to the souls, a complete analogy of the revolutions of all planets around the Sun, with the addition of time as a fourth spatial dimension. Sun at the centre of the system.

It is clear that this analogy has the Sun at the centre of the Solar System with all planets revolving around it, and thus it corresponds to the heliocentric model, which is accepted by modern science. It is supposed that Plato believed in the geocentric model or system, in which the Sun and all other bodies revolve around the Earth, which stands motionless at the centre of the world/Universe. Could it be that he knew or suspected the truth and used this metaphor to secretly convey to his readers his beliefs?

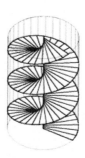

The helix of an internal staircase; however, the triremes probably had at best simple ladders for the oarsmen to ascend and descend to the rowing levels.

Of course, various claims have been publicised that certain ancient civilisations had astronomical knowledge that exceeded every imagination. In this vein, one could claim that Plato not only knows that the planets revolve around the Sun, but also the fact that the Sun is not motionless at the centre of the Universe (as the first heliocentrists, such as Aristarchus of Samos and Copernicus, believed), but instead it traces an almost straight trajectory, a fact that forces the planets to trace helixes in space. All these trajectories together resemble a luminous hyper-column and its grooves, very similar to a kind of helical "heavenly staircase" that connects the planets with the Sun and also the planets among themselves. Once again, this effect is produced from the integration in time of the motion of the Sun and of the planets that follow it, revolving around it. This whole system revolves around the centre of the Milky Way galaxy once every 225 to 250 million terrestrial years (the so-called galactic or cosmic year), so that the part of the Sun's trajectory traced in a few decades or even in a few centuries can be visualised as a straight line or a straight column, since it corresponds to an arc of the order of an arcsecond (specifically, one arcsecond of this galactic trajectory corresponds to about 180 years, which is longer than the period of any planet known in antiquity).

Naturally, equally surprising would be if Plato knew about the existence of the Van Allen radiation belts, or, even more, about the existence of the Edgeworth-Kuiper Belt in the remote edges of the Solar System. How could he possess all this specialised knowledge, which is not limited to the field of the science of astronomy, but it extends to psychology as well, since Plato seems in this metaphor to combine the function of our planetary system with the evolution of our souls? If this seems already impossible, then the reader should experience even more embarrassment in what follows, since the revelations of the myth of Er can be connected to modern science in a way that exceeds the most vivid human imagination

Chapter 7
THE SPINDLE OF NECESSITY

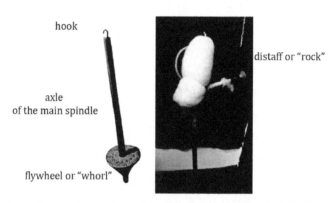

The main spindle consists of three parts: the flywheel ("whorl"), the spinning rod and the hook. There is also the distaff or "rock" (right-hand image).

Ἐκ δὲ τῶν ἄκρων τεταμένον ἀνάγκης ἄτρακτον, δι᾽ οὗ πάσας ἐπιστρέφεσθαι τὰς περιφοράς· οὗ τὴν μὲν ἠλακάτην τε καὶ τὸ ἄγκιστρον εἶναι ἐξ ἀδάμαντος, τὸν δὲ σφόνδυλον μεικτὸν ἔκ τε τούτου καὶ ἄλλων γενῶν. τὴν δὲ [616d] τοῦ σφονδύλου φύσιν εἶναι τοιάνδε· τὸ μὲν σχῆμα οἷάπερ ἡ τοῦ ἐνθάδε, νοῆσαι δὲ δεῖ ἐξ ὧν ἔλεγεν τοιόνδε αὐτὸν εἶναι, ὥσπερ ἂν εἰ ἐν ἑνὶ μεγάλῳ σφονδύλῳ κοίλῳ καὶ ἐξεγλυμμένῳ διαμπερὲς ἄλλος τοιοῦτος ἐλάττων ἐγκέοιτο ἁρμόττων, καθάπερ οἱ κάδοι οἱ εἰς ἀλλήλους ἁρμόττοντες, καὶ οὕτω δὴ τρίτον ἄλλον καὶ

131

τέταρτον καὶ ἄλλους τέτταρας. ὀκτὼ γὰρ εἶναι τοὺς σύμπαντας σφονδύλους, ἐν ἀλλήλοις ἐγκειμένους, [616e] κύκλους ἄνωθεν τὰ χείλη φαίνοντας, νῶτον συνεχὲς ἑνὸς σφονδύλου ἀπεργαζομένους περὶ τὴν ἠλακάτην· ἐκείνην δὲ διὰ μέσου τοῦ ὀγδόου διαμπερὲς ἐληλάσθαι. Ἐκ δὲ τῶν ἄκρων τεταμένον ἀνάγκης ἄτρακτον,...

And from the edges is stretched something like a spindle that owes its existence to the function of Necessity,...

... δι᾽ οὗ πάσας ἐπιστρέφεσθαι τὰς περιφοράς...

... through which all the orbits turn, twisting themselves like fibres.

....

At this point in the myth of Er appears for the first time the mysterious term "spindle of Necessity (*Ananke*)", which can be associated with Ananke (also spelled Anangke, Anance, or Anagke), the personification of Necessity in the ancient Greek religion and mythology, where she was regarded as the mother of the three Fates and the only person to have control over their decisions. However, according to the French scholar Guillaume Budé (Lat. *Guilielmus Budaeus*, 1467-1540) the phrase "spindle of Necessity" represents the celestial sphere of the fixed stars! Therefore, it can be said that here there is a connection or correlation of Greek mythology with astronomy referenced from as early as the European Renaissance. Indeed, the notion of necessity was exemplified with the inevitable apparent steady rotation of the celestial sphere of the distant, fixed stars around the

Earth (in reality, the Earth is the part that rotates around its own axis). On the other side, Ananke was, according to some mythological sources and, even more important, to the teachings of Pythagoras, one of the Protogenoi, the Greek primordial deities. Thus, Ananke marks the beginning of the cosmos, along with her father and consort, Chronos (= "time"), and she controls not only the creation of the Universe, but its particular functions as well, even its eventual fate. Some Greek philosophers seem to confuse it with Eimarmene, the subsequent personification of fate, fortune or predestination.

A parallel of the universal function of Ananke in modern physics can be found in the notion of entropy, a measure of the disorder present in any physical system, which, "inevitably", is "destined to" increase as time passes, although this is not required by any natural law.

Hence, the function of the Universe according to the Greeks is not the result of some decision of the Gods, but rather the result of the existence of this primordial entity or force: the ANANKE (the Greek word *ananke* means "compulsive" or natural necessity, and similarly in modern Greek it means also "need").

Thus, it is natural to suppose that the "spindle" described also moves according to the law of necessity, and not according to the laws of the Gods.

In order to understand the following, we should not forget that the hyper-column described in the previous chapter cannot be perceived under the conditions of the three-dimensional space in which we live, but only in the context of the fourth dimension of spacetime, which is time itself. The spindle is described as apparently stretched from the edges of the hyper-column.

... οὗ τὴν μὲν ἠλακάτην τε καὶ τὸ ἄγκιστρον εἶναι ἐξ ἀδάμαντος,...

... The distaff and the hook of this spindle are made of diamond [or they are of a similar nature],...

At this point there is a grand simile of the way our planetary system functions with the function of a distaff of a spindle, which spins raw wool in order to transform it into yarn (thread). Let us attempt to approach this simile.

It is known that the spinning of wool needs two distinct parts: A distaff (in Greek: *elakate*) and the main spindle. Both are necessary for processing the wool or other natural fibre and for producing the thread or yarn.

The distaff is the part where the raw fibre is fixed. The main spindle has two accessories, which are interconnected. The first one is the "whorl" or flywheel at its base and the second one is the hooked rod around which the yarn is wound.

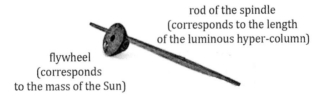

rod of the spindle
(corresponds to the length
of the luminous hyper-column)

flywheel
(corresponds
to the mass of the Sun)

The analogy between the spindle and the Solar System is the following: The flywheel corresponds to the mass of the Sun and of all the planets that revolve around it (the total mass of which is less than 0.2 percent of the Sun's mass). The rod corresponds to the bright pillar or hyper-column, which is produced by the light of the Sun.

However, in order for this "spindle of Necessity" to function in a proper way, the hooked rod and the distaff with the raw fibre must be always kept close together and interconnected to each other. The distaff itself is not a part of the main spindle, but rather an independent unit that provides the main spindle with the necessary raw material for the production of the processed thread, the yarn.

The distaff or rock (*elakate*) with the raw wool; it corresponds to the Kuiper belt.

Hence, the raw fibre, say white wool, could be compared to the orbits of the icy Kuiper belt objects (KBOs); for, as we have mentioned in the previous chapter, this belt contains the raw material that produces most of the comets, but only after its small objects become unstable; nowadays, astronomers believe that the so-called scattered disc objects (SDOs) at the exterior side (farther from the Sun) of the Kuiper belt, which have much more eccentric (elongated), dynamically unstable orbits than the KBOs, are the true source of the short-period comets we see in the inner Solar System.

The word "comet" itself in this case contributes to the analogy with its etymology: it comes from the Greek phrase "cometes aster", which means "star with hair", thus connecting comets with the notion of the raw fibre held by the distaff (wool is the hair of sheep).

According to the previous quotation of the ancient text of the *Republic*, the distaff has a crystalline nature like the diamond. Today, we actually know that the KBOs are made of various volatile materials in their crystalline solid form, in other words the ices of the materials that produce a comet's coma and tail (its "hair") if and when these *cometary nuclei* have their orbits changed and thus approach the Sun.

Now, a sizable proportion of these crystalline ices is water ice; water in its liquid form has been widely recognised in the last decades as the most necessary factor for the appearance of life as we know it, on any planet. Moreover, all comets contain organic compounds. Therefore, the "composition" of both the distaff and the hook as given by Plato points to the fact that in this planetary system living creatures, including humans, can appear; but only after this primal material undergoes processing by falling into the inner Solar System, i.e. metaphorically being transferred to the spinning rod, the main spindle, with the aid of the hook.

This processing in the case of the real spindle is the spinning of the wool into a yarn, while in the case of the Solar System is heating (thermal processing).

main spindle
(rod with hook)

raw wool

distaff or "rock"

processed yarn
(thread)

The raw wool held by the distaff or "rock" (upper right) is processed into yarn by spinning the main spindle (centre of the image).

We should concede that the whole process of pre-industrial yarn production is based on the flywheel or "whorl", which is attached in the lower edge of the main spindle rod (axle) and which secures for the rod an easily maintained roughly steady spinning rate.

Based on our previous unique metaphor for the coupling of the visible with the invisible world as revealed by Plato, we can compare the flywheel, which is the most massive part of the spindle, to the Sun and its mass, which keeps the whole Solar System in a state of perpetual moving equilibrium, through the gravitational attraction that exerts upon all its bodies, from the largest planet (Jupiter) to the smallest asteroid or Kuiper-belt object.

Additionally, we can compare the axle (hooked rod) of the main spindle to the central axis of the Solar System that passes from the centre of the Sun. Or to the vector of the motion of the Sun in space, following the arrow of time, forming an almost straight line around which the thread-orbit of each planet is wound in a helical form.

In the case of the spindle function, it is evident that without the flywheel the spinning of motion of the rod could not be retained and thus the raw material could neither be twisted into a yearn, nor wound on the rod. Correspondingly, in the case of the "function" of the Solar System, if the mass of the Sun did not dominate in its mass distribution, the planets could never form; and even if they existed, they could not orbit around the Sun.

In the first case the wool would never become yearn, while in the second case the original raw material of the solar nebula would never form the planetary system.

At the upper edge of the main spindle rod (axle) there is, as it has been described, a hook of the same adamantine nature, which we interpreted as crystalline in general. There is not known to modern science any other astronomical analogy for this "hook" one could suppose except from the hook of the force of gravity, the gravitational attraction between any two material bodies. Plato probably could offer us many other, non-scientific similes from his times.

The hook of gravity serves to both retain and stabilize the orbits of the planets and all other bodies of the Solar System around the Sun; and this while the Sun moves at a much greater speed on its trajectory around the centre of our Galaxy. The same force keeps the Sun itself on this trajectory (with all its planets anchored to their steady orbits around it) and indeed the whole Galaxy together. If we acknowledge that the rotation axis of the spindle corresponds to the Sun's trajectory in the interstellar space of the Galaxy, we should concede that this trajectory is not infinite, but it has a finite size, just as the rod of the spindle or the luminous hyper-column observed by the souls in the myth. Modern galactic dynamics assert that, although this trajectory is not exactly a closed curve, it remains a roughly circular path around the galactic centre.

Hence, this mysterious description by Plato can be linked to an interpretation of the function of the whole Solar System!

In the context of this metaphor between the function of a spindle and that of our planetary system, we should note that in our Solar System there are two separate "poles", one that controls the motion of its bodies and another that has to do with their origin. The second "pole" corresponds to the Kuiper belt, the distaff holding the raw material that once gave birth to planets and still gives birth to thousands of comets. The first pole is, of course, the Sun, which corresponds to the flywheel or the base upon which the rod of the spindle is attached. The Sun, because of its powerful gravitational field, forces all planets to obey to the Newton's law of universal gravitation by following their specific orbits around it.

Is there any other scientific metaphor we could consider for the thread of this spindle, apart from the planetary orbits? A well-known modern theory in fundamental physics is that of superstrings. According to this unproven theory, the elementary particles of matter have actually the form of strings in other, higher dimensions, which are curled to infinitesimal lengths. This reminds to us the extra dimension of the "hyper-column". The production of yearn by our spindle could then be paralleled to the creation of these strings from the quantum state that dominated during a practically infinitesimal part of the first trillionth of a second after the creation of the Universe according to the Big Bang theory.

As an ending note to this singular but consistent with reality metaphor, we add that, in the case of the man-made distaff, the raw wool or flax used in order to produce the processed yarn originates from the shearing of sheep or from the mowing of flax plants, respectively; in both cases, this is dead matter coming from a living organism. Similarly, the "raw" material of the Kuiper-belt objects originates from material that was ejected from older generations of stars that now are dead, mostly during the violent deaths, called supernova explosions, of stars much more massive than the Sun.

... τὸν δὲ σφόνδυλον μεικτὸν...

... while the flywheel is made of a material of a mixed [or blended] nature...

The flywheel is attached to the lower edge or base of the spindle; its "mixed nature" in our astronomical metaphor corresponds to its mixed, solar and planetary, origin. The nature of the Sun is different than the nature of the planets, since the Sun is a star, a celestial body that produces and emits its own light, while its planets just reflect the light they receive from the Sun. The Sun consists of hot ionized gas (gas composed of charged particles, both atomic nuclei and electrons, which move disconnected from one another), known as plasma, while all planets consist almost entirely of non-ionized matter (electrically neutral atoms) and a sizable portion of this matter, even in the case of the so-called "gaseous giant" planets, is in a solid or a liquid state. Aristotle would say that the Sun consists of an "aethereal" substance, while the planets are composed of the four classical Aristotelian elements.

Of course, we should concede that the Platonic description could offer more similes, if only we had a more advanced scientific level. Therefore, in the future, with the expected progress in the sciences, more and perhaps more successful metaphors could be discovered for this text.

There is an expression in modern Greek language that pertains exactly to this issue of understanding. It translates as "the sky hit me as a flywheel", and it is used in cases when a person gets suddenly dizzy after learning some very bad news, not necessarily in the strict medical sense, but usually metaphorically. In our Platonic metaphor, this corresponds to our limited ability to comprehend higher functions of the Universe.

... ἔκ τε τούτου καὶ ἄλλων γενῶν.

... of both this and other sorts of objects [cf. the Sun, planets and other celestial objects, such as asteroids].

Τὴν δὲ τοῦ σφονδύλου φύσιν εἶναι τοιάνδε:

As for the nature of the flywheel, we can describe it as follows:

... τὸ μὲν σχῆμα οἷάπερ ἡ τοῦ ἐνθάδε, νοῆσαι δὲ δεῖ ἐξ ὧν ἔλεγεν τοιόνδε αὐτὸν εἶναι,...

Its shape was that of the earthly ones, but from what Er said, we must understand that it is like...

... ὥσπερ ἂν εἰ ἐν ἑνὶ μεγάλῳ σφονδύλῳ κοίλῳ καὶ ἐξεγλυμμένῳ διαμπερὲς...

... if there is one great whorl, with a hollow interior, smooth and transparent,...

... ἄλλος τοιοῦτος ἐλάττων ἐγκέοιτο ἁρμόττων,...

... inside which there is enclosed another flywheel, similar but smaller in dimensions, fitting completely to the larger one...

... καθάπερ οἱ κάδοι οἱ εἰς ἀλλήλους ἁρμόττοντες...

... exactly as in the case of buckets that fit into one another [only that here there are transparent]...

... καὶ οὕτω δὴ τρίτον ἄλλον καὶ τέταρτον καὶ ἄλλους

τέτταρας.

... and in the same way fit a third, and a fourth, and four others [all of them inside the two previous ones].

We could better understand this description of nested flywheels by using as an example the well-known Russian matryoshka or "babushka" dolls. Coincidentally, Er is from Armenia, a region near the southern border of Russia, from where these dolls originally came (they are also known as Russian nesting dolls, or just Russian dolls).

A cross-sectional view of the nested flywheels (left), and a classical matryoshka doll set (right).

Ὀκτὼ γὰρ εἶναι τοὺς σύμπαντας σφονδύλους, ἐν ἀλλήλοις ἐγκειμένους,...

Because [we can say that] there are eight flywheels in total, lying within one another,...

... κύκλους ἄνωθεν τὰ χείλη φαίνοντας,...

...whose rims appear to be circular as observed from above,...

... νῶτον συνεχὲς ἑνὸς σφονδύλου ἀπεργαζομένους περὶ τὴν ἠλακάτην:

... while from below they appear to form all together the continuous back of a single flywheel, which revolves around the distaff;

At this point, Plato describes a majestic picture, which translates in modern astrophysical terms as follows: The orbits of the planets are readily visible as discrete if one could observe them from "above", while they cannot be discerned if one could observe them from "below"! What could this possibly mean?

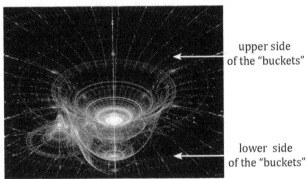

upper side
of the "buckets"

lower side
of the "buckets"

Let us remember the dimension of time with respect to this picture. We should understand that the "upper" side of the "buckets" corresponds to their "view" from future times; on the contrary, their "lower" side would be visible if we could observe them from the past. Therefore, this particular description could be seen as an illustration of the space bending or curving caused by the mass of the Sun (and of the planetary system in general).

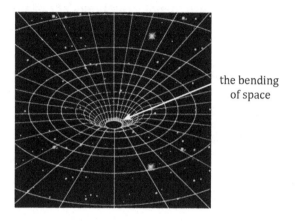

the bending of space

Indeed, probably the best possible metaphor that could lead to the understanding of the difficult notion of the space curvature is the example of an empty bucket: Observing it from above (the direction that corresponds to the future) we can see all its interior, down to its depths. But if we observe it from below its base (that is, from the past), we see only its exterior bottom surface and the exterior surface of its walls, without being able to observe its interior. The depths of the bucket correspond to the dimensions of space; from the past, we cannot see how this space will be like in the future.

Such observations could only be performed from a suitable distance and from an observer placed at the proper spacetime coordinates and conditions, which would offer an integrated perception of the whole planetary system. These observations could be done from a very distant point, far beyond the Kuiper belt. Such a remote point would be at the edges of the Solar System and its region would be what we call nowadays the Oort cloud, a theoretically predicted entity that, in a sense, defines the boundary of the Solar System.

The Oort cloud is divided into two regions, according to theorists: a disc-shaped inner Oort cloud (or Hills cloud) and a spherical outer Oort cloud. The outer sphere surrounds the entire Solar System. Thus, since the System's entire mass would be towards the same direction for an observer positioned outside of the outer Oort cloud, that observer could measure the curvature of this whole space (the interior of the largest "bucket") produced by the total mass of the Solar System.

Let us here remind that this bending of space is predicted by the general theory of relativity, whose last unverified prediction, the existence of gravitational waves, has been proved correct recently by the discovery of such waves coming from a merger of two black holes. Another development of the 2010s was the crossing of the heliopause by the NASA spacecraft *Voyager 1*, which had been launched as early as 20 August 1977. The heliopause is the border outside of which the magnetic field of the Sun, carried by the solar wind particles, is overpowered by the weak magnetic field of the Galaxy; accordingly, beyond this limit the solar wind succumbs to the pressure of the interstellar medium, the diffuse gas in the Milky Way Galaxy. In 2013, NASA announced that *Voyager 1* had crossed the heliopause on August 25, 2012. At that point the spacecraft was at a distance of 121 AU (Earth-Sun distances) or almost 17 light hours from the Sun; although it travels at a speed of 17 kilometres per second, it will take about 300 years to reach the Oort cloud and about 30,000 years to reach its outer limits.

The spacecraft Voyager 2, which is identical to Voyager 1.

There is a twin spacecraft that will soon cross the heliopause, *Voyager 2*, which is also destined to wander in the interstellar space, far beyond the Solar System. As of April 2015, *Voyager 2* was at a distance of 108 AU or 16,200,000,000 kilometres from the Sun, moving at a speed of approximately 3.2 AU per year. After 296,000 years, *Voyager 2* should pass by the star Sirius at a distance of 4.3 light-years!

Of course, in our parallel the human souls are much faster than these unmanned probes, as they need only 4 days to reach the Kuiper belt, which means that they travel at about 10 AU per day or a thousand times faster than even *Voyager 1!*

Our planetary system surrounded by the Kuiper belt and the Oort cloud.

The indisputable fact that the presence of mass "bends" space (it alters its geometry) could also be connected to the function of the mysterious "knee of Necessity", which is mentioned later in the text, as we will see in the next chapter.

... ἐκείνην δὲ διὰ μέσου τοῦ ὀγδόου διαμπερὲς ἐληλά-σθαι.

... and the distaff has passed its material through the middle of the eighth flywheel, and subsequently the material was transferred to the other flywheels.

This material of the distaff corresponds to the original, unprocessed (raw) material that formed the Solar System, which is still kept in its primal state in the Kuiper belt objects. Therefore, this passage carries us to the period of the formation of the solar planets. The eight flywheels (masses) can be readily identified in our metaphor as the eight planets of the Solar System: The innermost flywheel in the Platonic description is the smallest one. In complete analogy, planet Mercury is both the smallest of all eight planets and the innermost (nearest to the Sun) of all. (We should mention here, especially for the older readers, that Pluto was demoted to the status of "dwarf planet" by the International Astronomical Union in August 2006, so that there are now eight instead of nine planets in the Solar System.) Mercury is also the eighth planet measuring from the Kuiper belt to the Sun, the first one being Neptune.

In this context, the passage informs us that planet Mercury was the first one to be formed and subsequently the remaining material formed the other seven planets, including the Earth. Consequently, Mercury is connected with the strongest "thread" with the Sun, i.e. it is subjected to the strongest gravitational acceleration (the gravitational force per unit of its mass) by the Sun.

According to the other scientific metaphor we have mentioned earlier, we can alternatively compare each planet to a superstring, which oscillates at its own characteristic frequency. However, the superstring theory could be more appropriate in the last part of the following chapter, where each flywheel is associated with a distinct tone or musical sound, produced by a Siren.

Chapter 8
A DESCRIPTION OF THE PLANETS
AND THE KNEE OF NECESSITY

Τὸν μὲν οὖν πρῶτόν τε καὶ ἐξωτάτω σφόνδυλον πλατύτατον τὸν τοῦ χείλους κύκλον ἔχειν, τὸν δὲ τοῦ ἕκτου δεύτερον, τρίτον δὲ τὸν τοῦ τετάρτου, τέταρτον δὲ τὸν τοῦ ὀγδόου, πέμπτον δὲ τὸν τοῦ ἑβδόμου, ἕκτον δὲ τὸν τοῦ πέμπτου, ἕβδομον δὲ τὸν τοῦ τρίτου, ὄγδοον δὲ τὸν τοῦ δευτέρου. καὶ τὸν μὲν τοῦ μεγίστου ποικίλον, τὸν δὲ τοῦ ἑβδόμου λαμπρότατον, τὸν δὲ [617a] τοῦ ὀγδόου τὸ χρῶμα ἀπὸ τοῦ ἑβδόμου ἔχειν προσλάμποντος, τὸν δὲ τοῦ δευτέρου καὶ πέμπτου παραπλήσια ἀλλήλοις, ξανθότερα ἐκείνων, τρίτον δὲ λευκότατον χρῶμα ἔχειν, τέταρτον δὲ ὑπέρυθρον, δεύτερον δὲ λευκότητι τὸν ἕκτον. κυκλεῖσθαι δὲ δὴ στρεφόμενον τὸν ἄτρακτον ὅλον μὲν τὴν αὐτὴν φοράν, ἐν δὲ τῷ ὅλῳ περιφερομένῳ τοὺς μὲν ἐντὸς ἑπτὰ κύκλους τὴν ἐναντίαν τῷ ὅλῳ ἠρέμα περιφέρεσθαι, αὐτῶν δὲ τούτων τάχιστα μὲν ἰέναι τὸν ὄγδοον, δευτέρους δὲ καὶ ἅμα [617b] ἀλλήλοις τόν τε ἕβδομον καὶ ἕκτον καὶ πέμπτον· [τὸν] τρίτον δὲ φορᾷ ἰέναι, ὡς σφίσι φαίνεσθαι, ἐπανακυκλούμενον τὸν τέταρτον, τέταρτον δὲ τὸν τρίτον καὶ πέμπτον τὸν δεύτερον. στρέφεσθαι δὲ αὐτὸν ἐν τοῖς τῆς ἀνάγκης γόνασιν. ἐπὶ δὲ τῶν κύκλων αὐτοῦ ἄνωθεν ἐφ᾽ ἑκάστου βεβηκέναι Σειρῆνα

151

συμπεριφερομένην, φωνὴν μίαν ἱεῖσαν, ἕνα τόνον: ἐκ πασῶν δὲ ὀκτὼ οὐσῶν μίαν ἁρμονίαν συμφωνεῖν.

Τὸν μὲν οὖν πρῶτόν τε καὶ ἐξωτάτω σφόνδυλον πλατύτατον τὸν τοῦ χείλους κύκλον ἔχειν,...

So, the first and outermost flywheel [which is the largest one] has the broadest circular rim,...

From this point of the Platonic text starts an original analysis, which corresponds in our metaphor to a discussion of how an observer would see the orbits of the planets and the space between them, if that observer were placed in the Kuiper belt, as are the privileged souls, or even much further away, in the Oort cloud.

The discussion begins with the outermost flywheel, which corresponds to planet Neptune. For simplicity, we give the order of the planets as one would see them from the Kuiper belt, which is the following:

The first planet (the one closest to the Kuiper belt) is Neptune.

The second planet is Uranus.

The third planet is Saturn.

The fourth planet is Jupiter.

The fifth planet is Mars.

The sixth planet is the Earth.

The seventh planet is Venus.

The eighth planet is Mercury.

It is also important to comment further about the omission of Pluto. Apart from its demotion to the status of "dwarf planet" by the International Astronomical Union in 2006, is there any other reason to omit it? The orbit of Pluto is both more eccentric (that is, it deviates most from the circle) and much more inclined with respect to the ecliptic (the plane of the Earth's orbit around the Sun) than the orbit of any of the eight "proper" planets. Its large eccentricity results in the peculiar fact that around the perihelion of its orbit Pluto is closer to the Sun than planet Neptune; in other words, Pluto's orbit intersects the Neptunian orbit. Specifically, Pluto was closer to Sun than Neptune from 1979 to 1999. On the contrary, the Platonic text speaks about a circular rim of the outermost flywheel. Apart from this violation of the planetary order, the large inclination means that the flywheel of Pluto could not accommodate inside it the flywheels-"buckets" of the other planets.

Now, an observer positioned in the centre of the Kuiper belt would see Neptune to move across his or her field of view more than any other planet, covering a width of about 98 degrees; this corresponds to the external "broadest circular rim" of the Platonic text.

... τὸν δὲ τοῦ ἔκτου δεύτερον,...

...while the [rim] of the sixth [flywheel] was the second [broadest],...

....

The rim of the sixth flywheel has the second largest width of all; this in our analogy means that the orbit of the Earth is the second largest as seen from the Kuiper belt, which is wrong. The orbits of all planets are elliptical, not circular; however, they approach the perfect circle, as their eccentricities are very small (the circle can be defined as an ellipse with eccentricity e = 0). It is also true that the planetary orbits are not constant in time, since they are subject to perturbations caused by the gravity forces of the other planets.

... τρίτον δὲ τὸν τοῦ τετάρτου,...

...and that of the fourth was third,...

... τέταρτον δὲ τὸν τοῦ ὀγδόου,...

... that of the eighth was fourth,...

... πέμπτον δὲ τὸν τοῦ ἑβδόμου,...

... that of the seventh was fifth,...

... ἕκτον δὲ τὸν τοῦ πέμπτου,...

... that of the fifth was sixth,...

... ἕβδομον δὲ τὸν τοῦ τρίτου,...

..., that of the third was seventh,...

... ὄγδοον δὲ τὸν τοῦ δευτέρου.

... and that [the rim] of the second [flywheel] was the eighth [broadest].

Since the widths of the orbits do not correspond to their order mentioned here, is there any other analogy that could be employed here? Another possible interpretation of the ancient text could be the change in the size of each orbit with time. All the above orbits increase and decrease slightly in size in time scales of thousands of years, while they change completely in time scales of tens or hundreds of millions of years; the reason for both variations is the set of perturbations by the gravity of the rest of the planets. However, it is difficult to find out these increases and decreases; moreover, they do not remain the same in size for any given planet, so they are not a permanent numerical quantity for any given planet that could be ordered.

Apart from this, the two outermost planets need hundreds of years to complete just one orbit around the Sun, so that observations of many hundreds of years would be necessary in order to calculate the small variations of the average orbit. Plato would need advanced computing abilities and knowledge of celestial mechanics, plus observations that would span hundreds of years.

Καὶ τὸν μὲν τοῦ μεγίστου ποικίλον, τὸν δὲ τοῦ ἑβδόμου λαμπρότατον,...

And the rim of the greatest [i.e. the outermost] flywheel

is spangled [or multicoloured], while that of the seventh
[flywheel] is the brightest one;...

....

The outermost flywheel corresponds to the bluish planet Neptune, while the "seventh" planet, Venus, is indeed the brightest of the Solar System planets as seen from the Earth. However, in order to observe the exact colours and obtain precise brightness measurements of the planets, one should avoid the Earth's atmosphere. This can be done by observing either from the interplanetary space, or from the surface of a celestial body that has no atmosphere, like any small object of the Kuiper belt.

Of course, it is well-known that the planetary system presents many different colours and hues. Nowadays, we are lucky enough to be able to know the exact hues of the planets, from images taken by the Hubble Space Telescope, which operates above the atmosphere of the Earth. However, even the Earth-based casual observer can check the colour of the brighter planets.

... τὸν δὲ τοῦ ὀγδόου τὸ χρῶμα ἀπὸ τοῦ ἑβδόμου ἔχειν προσλάμποντος, τὸν δὲ τοῦ δευτέρου καὶ πέμπτου παραπλήσια ἀλλήλοις, ξανθότερα ἐκείνων, τρίτον δὲ λευκότατον χρῶμα ἔχειν, τέταρτον δὲ ὑπέρυθρον,...

... additionally, the eighth takes its colour from the seventh, which shines upon it; the colours of the second and fifth were similar and more yellow than the two former. The third [flywheel] had the whitest colour, and the

fourth was of a slightly reddish hue,...

In our analogy, the above are interpreted as follows: The planet Mercury takes its colour from Venus, which is logical, since Venus is much brighter than Mercury and relatively close to it. On the other hand, the colours of Uranus (second flywheel) and Mars (fifth) are said to be similar and lighter yellow than the former two; nothing could be farther from truth, as Uranus is light blue, while Mars is markedly reddish. Saturn is said to be the whitest planet, which is true if we compare it to its adjacent planets, Uranus and Jupiter; however, Venus is much more white in colour than Saturn. Finally, Jupiter does have reddish cloud bands, however, the surface of Mars as a whole is more reddish than these bands on Jupiter. Naturally, the famous Great Red Spot of Jupiter is larger than Earth and can be discerned even with good amateur telescopes from our planet; yet, it is not a permanent feature: it is known to exist for a couple of hundred years and it is not known whether it has lived ten times as much. that is whether it existed in Plato's times.

... δεύτερον δὲ λευκότητι τὸν ἕκτον.

...while the second in whiteness was the sixth one.

In our metaphor, the second brightest planet (after Saturn 0.342) is said to be our own planet, the Earth. In reality, Earth as seen from space is on the average slightly whiter than Saturn, but this is because of its clouds, which of

157

course vary widely in extent; the oceans are much darker with their deep blue colour. On the other hand, all the visible surface of Saturn consists of clouds, but these do not vary considerably on a global scale.

Κυκλεῖσθαι δὲ δὴ στρεφόμενον τὸν ἄτρακτον ὅλον μὲν τὴν αὐτὴν φοράν,...

[We should, on the other hand, consider that] the whole spindle [which consists of all the flywheels and the axle] rotates around its axis circularly in the same sense (way of rotation),...

... ἐν δὲ τῷ ὅλῳ περιφερομένῳ τοὺς μὲν ἐντὸς ἑπτὰ κύκλους τὴν ἐναντίαν τῷ ὅλῳ ἠρέμα περιφέρεσθαι,...

... but when somebody observes the rotation of the whole system from the outside, the seven inner circles rotate gently in the opposite direction to the whole ,...

This information is held by other commentators as well (for example Burnet), to correspond to the orbital motion (revolution) of the planets. Indeed, as seen from the Earth all other planets seem to move from time to time in the opposite direction, an effect produced by the orbital motion of the Earth itself. To this we could just add the slow revolution of the Kuiper belt objects (KBOs) around the Sun: since the KBOs revolve slowly around the Sun in the same direction as the planets, the motion of the latter would appear slower or more "gentle" as seen from the surface of a KBO.

... αὐτῶν δὲ τούτων τάχιστα μὲν ἰέναι τὸν ὄγδοον,...

... and of these seven the eighth moved most swiftly,...

... δευτέρους δὲ καὶ ἅμα ἀλλήλοις τόν τε ἕβδομον καὶ ἕκτον καὶ πέμπτον:...

... and next and together with one another the seventh, sixth and fifth;...

Nowadays the revolution speeds of the planets around the Sun are known with excellent precision. As described by Plato, the eighth planet as seen from the Kuiper belt, namely Mercury, revolves with the greatest speed of all eight, 47.4 kilometres per second on the average, followed by Venus (the seventh planet), the Earth (the sixth one), and Mars (the fifth one). Mercury revolves around the Sun once every 88 days. Venus revolves once every 225 days, moving at an average speed of 35.0 km per second. Earth revolves once every 365.26 days, moving at 29.8 km/sec. Mars revolves once every 687 days, moving at 24.1 km/sec on the average. Hence, the Platonic description accords absolutely with reality.

... [τὸν] τρίτον δὲ φορᾷ ἰέναι,...

... and as far the motion of the third one is concerned,...

... ὡς σφίσι φαίνεσθαι, ἐπανακυκλούμενον τὸν τέταρτον,...

... it appeared to them that it revolved much more slowly than the fourth one, which returns upon it,...

The planet Saturn, which corresponds to the third flywheel, revolves around the Sun once every 10,759 days, moving at an average speed of only 9.7 km per second relative to the Sun; this is much slower than the motion of Jupiter, which revolves around the Sun once every 4,333 days with an average speed of 13.1 km/sec. In other words, Jupiter completes more than two revolutions around the Sun at the same period of time that Saturn completes one; this is the meaning of the phrase "returns upon it".

... τέταρτον δὲ τὸν τρίτον...

... while the third one is the fourth in speed...

... καὶ πέμπτον τὸν δεύτερον.

... and the second one is the fifth in speed.

At this point of the text a new order appears; it can be correlated with the planetary speeds only if we assume that our own planet, the Earth is the measurement standard. Thus, the third planet, Saturn, is the fourth in order of decreasing speed beginning from the Earth as number one; similarly, the second planet from the Kuiper belt, Uranus, is the fifth in speed. Additionally, Mars is second in speed after the Earth and Jupiter is the third in speed. Uranus revolves around the Sun once every 30,689 days with an average orbital speed of only 6.8 km/sec.

Once again we note that Plato does not mention a ninth flywheel, which would correspond to the dwarf planet Pluto. As we explained, besides its much smaller mass and size, its orbit is much more irregular than the orbit of any other planet, so its "bucket" would not fit the "bucket" of the planet Neptune inside it (remember that their orbits cross each other). Although both the tiny mass and the irregular orbit of Pluto were known for several decades, its demotion to the status of "dwarf planet" by the International Astronomical Union came only as late as in 2006; this decision was taken for an additional, equally compelling, reason: The discovery of the dwarf planet Eris in the previous year, which has a greater mass than Pluto and almost the same size, being also a trans-Neptunian object, precipitated the decision, since it was reasonably argued that several more trans-Neptunian objects of comparable size and mass would be discovered in the future.

Subsequently, in June 2008 the International Astronomical Union introduced the term "plutoids" to describe all trans-Neptunian objects that are large enough in size to be classified as dwarf planets, i.e. to have an almost spherical shape because of their self-gravity. A more descriptive synonym in common use is "ice dwarfs". The official criterion of differentiating between a planet and a dwarf planet is more subtle: A planet has enough gravity to have "cleared the neighbourhood" around its orbit while a dwarf planet has not; in other words, any other object in the same or similar orbit with a given planet is either a satellite of that planet, has collided with it or has been ejected after a close enough encounter with the planet in the past. Thus, the gravity of a planet is strongly felt in a much more extended region of space than the gravity of a dwarf planet.

If these recent developments had not taken place, then obviously the analogy of the eight flywheels of the ancient text with the eight planets of the Solar System would not exist. Alternatively, today there are only four bodies verified to be plutoids: Pluto itself, Eris, Haumea, and Makemake; however, it is almost certain that many more exist, probably about 70 among the trans-Neptunian objects that have been already discovered. If, therefore we extended the Platonic scheme up to the level of our current knowledge, we would speak of 13 flywheels or "buckets", which would correspond to the 8 planets and the 5 dwarf planets of the Solar System (the four plutoids plus Ceres of the Main asteroid belt). However, the number 13 is not mentioned anywhere in the text of the Myth of Er.

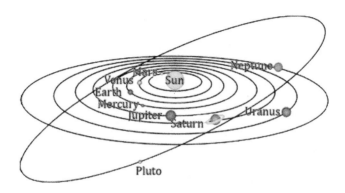

The irregular orbit of Pluto, both highly inclined to the orbits of the 8 planets and with a larger eccentricity, shows that its "bucket" would not fit those of the ordinary 8 planets inside it.

Στρέφεσθαι δὲ αὐτὸν ἐν τοῖς τῆς ἀνάγκης γόνασιν.

Apart from that, [the second flywheel] turns on the knees of Necessity.

At this point, the verb used by the philosopher (in the grammatical form of infinitive in the prototype) changes: instead of "moving", we have "turning". This should correspond to the rotation or spinning of the planets around their own axes, instead of their revolution around the Sun, to which the previous section was devoted.

Then, an extremely interesting analogy appears in the case of the second planet, which is Uranus: It is long known to astronomers that this large planet rotates almost perpendicularly to its orbit around the Sun, a characteristic that is unique among all planets. In other words, the Uranian axis of rotation is tilted sideways, nearly into the plane of its orbit. Its north and south poles therefore lie where most other planets have their equators. This almost right angle of axial tilt (more precisely it is equal to 82.23 degrees compared to the 90 degrees of a right angle) would be aptly compared as appearing to form a "knee". No other planet comes close to that value; Neptune comes second with an axial tilt of 28.3 degrees, while Earth has a tilt of 23.44 degrees, called the obliquity of the ecliptic, which produces the four seasons of the year.

This means that Uranus moves "kneeling" around the Sun; it has also been described as "rolling" on its orbit around the Sun, but the latter simile is true only at or near its solstices. Could Uranus be further described as the victim of a "Necessity"? The reason for the unusual axial tilt is not known with certainty, but a common speculation is that during the formation of the Solar System, an Earth-sized protoplanet collided with Uranus, causing its unique "kneeled" orientation.

Interestingly, in astrology Uranus is connected to the property of disrupting the inertness. It could be argued that this is exactly what happened when the primal large body collided with Uranus, more than four billion years ago. This unique "fate" of planet Uranus reminds us that the personification of Necessity in the ancient Greek mythology was regarded as the mother of the three Fates and the only person to have control over their decisions.

Fate is intimately connected with the passing of time, and thus the mention of the unique feature of Uranus can be associated to the metaphor in Chapter 6 of the four-dimensional "hyper-column" that represents the planetary orbits through time as the fourth dimension. The space is bent by the presence of the mass of the Sun and the planets, while Uranus has been bent to a "kneeling position" by the collision of a massive body. Advancing the ideas of Greek philosophy, one could theorise that Necessity, also associated with the inevitability of entropy, defines the arrow of time, differentiating the past from the future, and thus it produces and regulates the function of spacetime.

In human anatomy the knee is the joint that plays the basic role in movement of the body related to both horizontal (running and walking) and vertical (jumps) directions, exactly as the two motions (revolution and rotation) of Uranus are approximately in a "horizontal" and a "vertical" direction — in scientific terminology, the angular momentum vector of Uranus due to its rotation is almost perpendicular to its angular momentum vector due to its revolution around the Sun.

On the other hand, let us not forget that in a certain line of symbolism the legs represent the main symbol of the soul! Thus, it could be argued that, since the knee is the basic motional joint of the leg, it symbolises the motional directioning of the soul. The abstract notion of necessity is what forces the souls to reincarnate. The planetary system, since it bends space (actually this is done almost entirely the Sun by itself), symbolically defines necessity for humans and their souls; the fate-necessity that dictates the time of the creation and birth of each one of us, as well as the time of our death, a parallel to the creation and the death of the planets. Here we should also remember the aforementioned association of Necessity with entropy.

However, probably the most intriguing point, which attracts the attention immediately, is that the visual description of the "knee of Necessity" is essentially the same with that of the bottom of the four-dimensional "bucket", in other words of the bending of space caused mainly by the Sun as seen from the Kuiper belt.

At this point, let us attempt once more a "wordplay decoding" with the Greek word GONY = knee. The few letters of this word are enough to hide in them the G-enesis of NOY (*nou* = "of the mind" in both ancient and modern Greek). Like the curvature of space, this also implies the origin of matter, since, in order to appear, mind needs necessarily the brain, an organ made of matter, and hence the birth (in Greek *gennesis*) of a human. In this context, the Knee of Necessity can be said to create matter itself and, through, it the bending of space, something that is supported by the personification of Necessity (Ananke in Greek) as the mythical mother of the three Fates, which decide about the past, the present and the future!

After all these correlations, a new picture emerges, as we understand the reason for the appearance of the "buckets" from different aspects. When we observe them from above, we see both the rim of the planetary orbits and the interior, while from below we see only the bottom and not the interior, because of the curvature of space, which in turn is a result of concentrations of matter and of the MOTION OF THE TIME ARROW. This motion is visualised as the luminous hyper-column, which contains the mass of the

Sun and its planets.

The Kuiper belt, because of its considerable distance from the Sun, has an advantageous view of the system of the eight planets in its entirety, and not just that: because of the considerable thickness of the Kuiper belt, an observer placed inside it could see both the upper side and the underside of that system of planets, depending on the observer's position. Similarly, the privileged souls that reach the Kuiper belt can metaphorically observe both the bending of space and its evolution through time. By this it is also indicated that the soul can move both faster and more slowly than the arrow of time.

This is the reason that the evolved souls of the just have the right to move to what corresponds to the Kuiper Belt, since from there they can experience the curvature of space and even probably the expansion of the Universe, which we could say would assist them in deciding about their future itinerary towards their final destination: the Isles of the Blessed.

Ἐπὶ δὲ τῶν κύκλων αὐτοῦ ἄνωθεν ἐφ' ἐκάστου βεβη-κέναι Σειρῆνα συμπεριφερομένην, φωνὴν μίαν ἱεῖ-σαν, ἕνα τόνον:

And above each of these circles [formed by the rims of the spindle's flywheels] stands a Siren, revolving along with them and uttering one sound, one note;

... ἐκ πασῶν δὲ ὀκτὼ οὐσῶν μίαν ἁρμονίαν συμφωνεῖν.

... and by all the eight [frequencies emitted by the] Sirens is produced the concord of one single harmony.

In other words, there are eight "musical notes", which determine the "harmony of the celestial spheres" that Pythagoras has been said to hear. Each Siren participates in the revolution of each planet along its orbit (circular rim), which means that she is positioned on the planet's surface. And each Siren emits a "sound" signal of different frequency for each flywheel-planet. Moreover, these eight notes are separated by harmonic intervals. There is, of course, a caveat about the "sound" nature of these tones: It is well-known that sound cannot propagate in outer space, since its waves are material density waves that propagate through matter.

More imaginatively, we could think of these eight tones of the Sirens as produced by vibrations of superstrings, in which case they would be characterised as the "eigenfrequencies" or natural frequencies of each string-Siren. These superstrings are like the strings of a violin; their difference is that their vibrations, instead of producing musical notes, produce elementary particles.

As a conclusion, we could imagine that these Sirens sing and the "sounds" derive from the pulse produced when a superstring or the "yearn" of the orbit of a given planet vibrates.

The obliquity of the rotational axis of planet Uranus corresponds to the notion of the "knee of Necessity".

Chapter 9
THE THREE FATES

A relief of the three Fates or Moirai (Clotho, Lachesis and Atropos) by
Johann Gottfried Schadow at the Old National Gallery, Berlin.

Ἄλλας δὲ καθημένας [617c] πέριξ δι᾽ ἴσου τρεῖς, ἐν θρόνῳ
ἑκάστην, θυγατέρας τῆς ἀνάγκης, Μοίρας, λευχειμονούσας,
στέμματα ἐπὶ τῶν κεφαλῶν ἐχούσας, Λάχεσίν τε καὶ Κλωθὼ
καὶ Ἄτροπον, ὑμνεῖν πρὸς τὴν τῶν Σειρήνων ἁρμονίαν,
Λάχεσιν μὲν τὰ γεγονότα, Κλωθὼ δὲ τὰ ὄντα, Ἄτροπον δὲ
τὰ μέλλοντα. καὶ τὴν μὲν Κλωθὼ τῇ δεξιᾷ χειρὶ ἐφαπτομένην
συνεπιστρέφειν τοῦ ἀτράκτου τὴν ἔξω περιφοράν,
διαλείπουσαν χρόνον, τὴν δὲ Ἄτροπον τῇ ἀριστερᾷ τὰς
ἐντὸς αὖ ὡσαύτως· τὴν δὲ Λάχεσιν [617d] ἐν μέρει ἑκατέρας
ἑκατέρᾳ τῇ χειρὶ ἐφάπτεσθαι. σφᾶς οὖν, ἐπειδὴ ἀφικέσθαι,
εὐθὺς δεῖν ἰέναι πρὸς τὴν Λάχεσιν. προφήτην οὖν τινα σφᾶς
πρῶτον μὲν ἐν τάξει διαστῆσαι, ἔπειτα λαβόντα ἐκ τῶν τῆς

Λαχέσεως γονάτων κλήρους τε καὶ βίων παραδείγματα, ἀναβάντα ἐπί τι βῆμα ὑψηλὸν εἰπεῖν...

Ἄλλας δὲ καθημένας πέριξ δι' ἴσου τρεῖς,...

But there are also another three women, who are seated at equal distances between one another around the outermost ring;...

It is quite impressive that the above description by Plato corresponds to another characteristic situation in the Solar System, which is a general property of three-body gravitating systems that has been proved through celestial mechanics.

The only arrangement for three points on the circumference of a circle to be at equal distances between any two of them is to form three angles of 120 degrees.

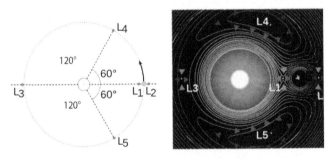

The symmetrical positions of the Lagrangian points around the Sun.

Indeed, it is known to astronomers that for any given planetary orbit there are three points at equal distances from each other, at which a body of negligible mass compared to that of the planet and the Sun is at equilibrium. These very special positions, along with two others, are called "Lagrangian points".

Jupiter, as the most massive planet, is the best example, since at the two stable Lagrangian points of its orbit around the Sun, L4 and L5, there are actually thousands of asteroids, which have been dynamically locked at their vicinity. These two points along with L3 are the three points at equal distances from each other mentioned above: L4 and L5 precede and follow (respectively) the planet on its orbit by 60 degrees, while L3 lies at 180 degrees from Jupiter. The other two Lagrangian points, L1 and L2, are outside of the orbit and much closer to the planet, so that for our discussion we could say that they coincide with the position of the planet itself.

Of these five points, only L4 and L5 are points of stable equilibrium, so that any celestial body that happens to pass from their vicinity can remain there forever, preceding or following the orbit of the planet. Astronomers call these bodies "Trojan" asteroids or trojan objects. The trojan asteroids are not satellites of the planet, since they do not revolve around it, and cannot collide with the planet. The first Jupiter trojan was discovered in 1906, the first Mars trojan in 1990 and the first Neptune trojan in 2001. Uranus has only one known trojan asteroid, discovered in 2011. Our own planet, Earth (more precisely, the Earth-Moon system), has also one known trojan, discovered on 1 October 2010 by NASA's WISE spacecraft, which precedes Earth in its orbit around the Sun, oscillating around L4.

The term "trojan" itself originated from the custom of naming Jupiter trojans after warriors of the Trojan War; the Jupiter trojans in the region of L4, which precede the planet by 60 degrees, are named after Greek warriors (hence the term "Greek camp"), while the Jupiter trojans in the region of L5, which follow the planet by 60 degrees, are named after Trojan warriors (hence the term "Trojan camp"). There are only two exceptions to this rule, named before the tradition was set, known as "spies": 624 Hektor in the Greek camp and 617 Patroclus in the Trojan camp.

From these astronomical facts we can conclude that the three points at which the three women of the myth are stationed are have their actual counterparts in the form of the Lagrangian points L3, L4, and L5. These women are promptly identified in the text as the three Fates (Moirai in Greek):

ἐν θρόνῳ ἑκάστην,...

... these women sit each one on her throne,...

... θυγατέρας τῆς ἀνάγκης, Μοίρας,...

... and they are the three Fates, daughters of Necessity (Ananke);...

According to the mechanics of the Lagrangian points, these equilibrium points can be described as "thrones", because they never change their distance from the planet to which they correspond. Therefore, any inert object placed there remains stationary with respect to the planet, although it does revolve around the Sun, and can theoretically stay at these points forever.

As it was mentioned earlier, the notion of Necessity can be compared with the notion of entropy in physics and biology. Thus, it could be said that on these three Fates depends the entropy of the terrestrial beings, which is a measure of the age, or the distance between birth and death.

It is obvious that the eight Sirens of the previous chapter correspond to the eight notes of the musical scale, since each Siren emits its distinct tone or frequency. In this case, the three Fates could be metaphors for the three musical clefs. In the theory of music, the clef is a symbol placed at the beginning of each stave that is used to indicate the name of written notes according to their place on the stave. Based on the clef that is written on a given stave, a musician can identify the notes that correspond to the to its lines and line intervals.

In other words, every note symbol on the stave can express a different note, which depends on the clef that appears at the stave's beginning; the same note symbol can change its pitch according to the clef.

In a metaphor to human life, the same musical composition could produced different emotions to each person; these emotions would depend on the clef according to which the music would be played and would not be the same. The difference would depend on the evolution of each person's soul.

The three Fates could be correlated to the three clefs that exist in musical notation as follows:

Each of these clefs is used for different instruments and voices, depending on the range of tones (*tessitura*) for each instrument; so the use of different clefs makes it possible to write music for all instruments and voices. Generally speaking, the G-clef is used for high parts, the C-clef for middle parts, and the F-clef for low parts. In the above analogy with the human soul, an unevolved soul wants to hear the low pitches or parts, while an evolved soul wants to hear the high parts.

... λευχειμονούσας,...

... they wear white vestments...

Because the white "colour" is composed from all frequencies or "pitches" of visible light, it is considered as a neutral colour.

This means metaphorically that the Fates themselves have no responsibility on the subject of which of the three we will choose as a priority in our life; that is, if we once decide that the clef under which we hear the music does not satisfy us, we have the undeniable right to choose another one.

… στέμματα ἐπὶ τῶν κεφαλῶν ἐχούσας,…

… and crowns or headbands on their heads;…

Here we should accept the interpretation that, since the three Fates wear crowns, they function as queens in our lives. Depending on which one we will choose to follow, she will unlock with her *clef* (French for "key") the path of our evolution.

Philosophically, the existence of the three Fates is connected with the issues of the Free Will and of the general evolution of the human soul, which is examined in the following chapters. However, at this point the text reveals some necessary preliminary information.

… Λάχεσίν τε καὶ Κλωθὼ καὶ Ἄτροπον, ὑμνεῖν πρὸς τὴν τῶν Σειρήνων ἁρμονίαν,…

… their names are Lachesis, and Clotho, and Atropos, and they sing hymns according to the music emitted by the Sirens.

In our analogy, it should be clear that this transcendental music, upon reaching each person's ears, will influence him or her according to the clef of the particular Fate he or she follows.

Incidentally, the notion of the "thrones" can be interpreted as the control by the three Lagrangian points of the three facets of time, that is the past, the future and the present:

... Λάχεσιν μὲν τὰ γεγονότα, Κλωθὼ δὲ τὰ ὄντα, Ἄτροπον δὲ τὰ μέλλοντα.

Lachesis sings the things that were, Clotho the things that are, and Atropos the things that are to be.

This means that, if we follow Lachesis, then we will remain and repeat the events of the past, being in a sense absolutely "fatal", playthings in the hands of fate. If we follow Clotho, then we will function as living intelligent beings, being able to take our fate in our own hands. If we follow Atropos, we will probably be capable of predicting the future, like Pythia, the Oracle of Delphi.

An underlying meaning for the myth of the three Fates is to understand that we should escape from the predestined path of our life, which is associated with the choice of Lachesis, who keeps us chained on the past, having signed the contract of our reincarnation along with us, as it will be mentioned later.

Clotho determines how humans will interpret in present time the meaning and the role of the past; in this context, she determines the extent to which they will manage to use their free will. In these decisions, the Greeks were considerably assisted by the ancient mysteries, especially the "Descent to Hades" of the Eleusinian Mysteries.

Atropos determines the future of humans depending on the way they perform their roles; this was the gift of Apollo, who gave the prophecy powers to each Pythia.

Hence we conclude that, according to Plato, the actions of our lives can be differentiated according to the "clef" of the three Fates we use. In the same way a given musical note changes its tone depending on the clef we use, the acts of one's life can change their meaning. Each action within a role is predetermined and corresponds to a certain melody. The choice of the clef we will use in order to perform this melody depends on us. We have three alternatives with respect to the interpretation of the same predetermined melody, which is a part of our role:

1) A bad interpretation, due to the inadequacies of our soul, symbolised by the F-clef of Lachesis.

2) A satisfying interpretation, which is what we want and is symbolised by the C-clef of Clotho.

3) An interpretation which is "too good" and is symbolised by the G-clef of Atropos.

Καὶ τὴν μὲν Κλωθὼ τῇ δεξιᾷ χειρὶ ἐφαπτομένην συνεπιστρέφειν τοῦ ἀτράκτου τὴν ἔξω περιφοράν,...

And Clotho with the touch of her right hand turns the spindle in the opposite direction (i.e. clockwise), so that its outer circumference [which corresponds to the most recently produced part of the yearn] is unfolded,...

... διαλείπουσαν χρόνον,...

... a procedure during which the [Arrow of] time stops,...

There is a theory in quantum mechanics according to which time itself is quantized, so that Clotho could interrupt its flow by blocking its feeding with discrete quanta (its smallest possible, indivisible spans). One could possibly interpret this passage by arguing that what Clotho spins is the feeding of time itself. Remember that Clotho stands for the present time and the free will.

... τὴν δὲ Ἄτροπον τῇ ἀριστερᾷ τὰς ἐντὸς αὖ ὡσαύτως...

... while Atropos with her left hand in like manner helps to turn the inner circles anticlockwise;...

Atropos, who represents the future, using her left hand, causes time to resume its flow or "normal function": all the planets of the Solar System revolve around the Sun anticlockwise. However, she does so only after Clotho is over and the next reincarnation must begin. The corollary is that, as long as the soul remains without a body, there is no ("planetary") time for it: the soul is timeless with respect to the time of our Universe.

... τὴν δὲ Λάχεσιν ἐν μέρει ἑκατέρας ἑκατέρᾳ τῇ χειρὶ ἐφάπτεσθαι.

... but as for Lachesis, she can use both her right and her left hand.

Lachesis, who represents the past, can use her right hand to stop the flow of time (like Clotho) and her left hand to restart this flow (like Atropos). This is because the past represents the incarnated phase of a soul's life: In our human lives on Earth we mostly think about the past, being able to remember all the important past events and, according to some people, even to obtain information from our past lives through meditation. On the other "hand", the Greeks believed that we can also obtain information from the future, by asking the oracles; thus, we could handle both directions of time, clockwise and anticlockwise.

Σφᾶς οὖν, ἐπειδὴ ἀφικέσθαι,...

Now when the souls arrived, ...

... εὐθὺς δεῖν ἰέναι πρὸς τὴν Λάχεσιν.

... they had to go immediately before Lachesis;...

Since Lachesis essentially controls the flow of time, this passage can be interpreted to mean that we should immediately begin the study of our souls by attempting to understand the way Lachesis operates. For the past incorporates the only measurable time spans that can be perceived by humans: the present and the future are impossible to measure.

Προφήτην οὖν τινα σφᾶς πρῶτον μὲν ἐν τάξει διαστῆσαι,...

...so then a certain prophet first separated and arranged them in orderly intervals,...

Lachesis, therefore, is the one Fate who, by stopping the arrow of time, gives the opportunity to each soul separately to become a "prophet". This is the first task every soul has to execute, so that the soul will organise the life of the next reincarnation in an orderly way, when the time of that reincarnation starts to flow and to be measured. Lachesis offers to each soul in advance the opportunity to discern the errors of the past, whatever wrongdoing was perpetrated during all the previous reincarnations up to this point (which usually we have the tendency to repeat in the present life). On the other hand, Lachesis in addition offers the souls the opportunity to discern the consequences their present actions will have in the future.

"Prophet" becomes every soul that comes into contact with Lachesis and remembers the past but also acquires the unique capability to see the consequences of a wrong life in the future. Thus, the souls understand all the errors they have done in their previous lives and have the tendency to repeat in future lives, while with the prophetic capability they can choose a suitable future life, so that will live a life that will allow them to have a good future evolution.

It is not a coincidence that the Greek maxim *gnōthi s'auton* (= "know thyself") is an advice inscribed in the forecourt of the Temple of Apollo at Delphi: For the Greek thought, the approach of the knowledge of the self was associated with the concept of becoming a prophet; each one should become the prophet of his or her own future; in this way we would be able to put our lives (either the present or future ones) in an order. A physicist would parallel this by saying that to become a prophet is to achieve a state of minimum entropy.

... ἔπειτα λαβόντα ἐκ τῶν τῆς Λαχέσεως γονάτων κλήρους τε καὶ βίων παραδείγματα,...

... *and after that they (or the prophet) took from the knees of Lachesis lots and patterns of lives,...*

... ἀναβάντα ἐπί τι βῆμα ὑψηλὸν εἰπεῖν,...

... *and went up to some kind of elevated platform and spoke as follows:...*

Now these souls have first to examine the lots received from the knees of the Fate, which have to do with various opportunities of reincarnation for their next lives, and afterwards they will have to ascend to the "orator's podium", that is to be heard by all, in order to make the statement of the following chapter.

Chapter 10
A "CONTRACT OF REINCARNATION"

...«ἀνάγκης θυγατρὸς κόρης Λαχέσεως λόγος. Ψυχαὶ ἐφήμεροι, ἀρχὴ ἄλλης περιόδου θνητοῦ γένους θανατηφόρου. [617e] οὐχ ὑμᾶς δαίμων λήξεται, ἀλλ᾽ ὑμεῖς δαίμονα αἱρήσεσθε. πρῶτος δ᾽ ὁ λαχὼν πρῶτος αἱρείσθω βίον ᾧ συνέσται ἐξ ἀνάγκης. ἀρετὴ δὲ ἀδέσποτον, ἣν τιμῶν καὶ ἀτιμάζων πλέον καὶ ἔλαττον αὐτῆς ἕκαστος ἕξει. αἰτία ἑλομένου· θεὸς ἀναίτιος.»

... «ἀνάγκης θυγατρὸς κόρης Λαχέσεως λόγος.

"These are the terms [for reincarnation] set by Lachesis, the maiden daughter of Necessity:...

This "oration" of each soul (or of the prophet, according to the standard translation) constitutes the "contract" each soul "signs" before its reincarnation with Lachesis, just the two of them. The "signing" of this agreement is a prerequisite in order for the soul to use the lot of the next reincarnation taken from the knees of Lachesis. The soul or the prophet ascends on an elevated podium in order to attach to this promise the greatest formality and solemnity.

The soul must publicly announce that acknowledges the rules and the terms of the next reincarnation; in this way, when the moment of death will come, the soul will not present some absurd claim, as we have seen before in the case of the wicked souls of the private citizens, who considered that they could enter the gate to ascend to the "outer Van Allen belt".

The agreement consists of seven terms, which are announced by the soul in the exact form they are communicated by Lachesis herself.

Ψυχαὶ ἐφήμεροι,...

1. Souls are ephemeral (they live on Earth for a number of terrestrial days).

It is clear that the soul without a body is immortal, while an reincarnated soul is subject to the event of the body's death; the reincarnated souls, to which the above phrase applies, can lose their mortal body at any moment. The immortal souls are forced by the function of the three Fates to be reincarnated as many times as it is judged to be necessary, until they manage to achieve their integration, the completion of their evolution. This means that the souls will be led to the achievement of their *entelecheia*, which will result in the immortality of the future bodies they will reside in.

... ἀρχὴ ἄλλης περιόδου θνητοῦ γένους θανατηφόρου.

*2. Now is the beginning of another cycle of mortal gen-
eration, where birth is the carrier of death.*

Each reincarnation is the start of a different life, which,
however, will also inescapably end with death, as long as
the soul continues to belong to a mortal rank.

Here we should remind to the reader that, according to
the theory of human evolution formulated by Aristotle, our
entity can belong to one of three different such "ranks".
Both the first and the second of these ranks, namely the
humanoid and the human, are mortal. Only the third rank,
that of the "self-human", is immortal, and our evolution into
that rank should be the main target of each reincarnation.

We must understand that the soul, according to this narration, "signs" at the beginning of each reincarnation the
analogue of a death contract with the Fate Lachesis. So
every new reincarnated life must strive for the evolution of
the *logistikon* of the soul's *trimereia* (see Chapter 3). If the
full restoration of the *logistikon*, the *"technosis* of the mind"
of the Aristotelian philosophers, is not achieved, then we
fail to achieve the purpose of our life and the result is the
inevitable death, in other words the separation of the soul
from the body.

The task of Lachesis is to keep administering lots, i.e. new
opportunities of reincarnation to any given soul, until this
soul manages to achieve the common final target for all
souls, which is the integrated function of the *trimereia* that

will bring along with it the common immortality of both soul and body.

Οὐχ ὑμᾶς δαίμων λήξεται,...

3. The reason for your death is not the decision of a certain daemon;...

... ἀλλ' ὑμεῖς δαίμονα αἰρήσεσθε.

... on the contrary, you will choose your own daemon [who fits your quality and who will be forced at some moment to end your life].

Each soul attracts a demon by living in an unsuccessful manner and making wrong choices as an embodied entity. It seems that every reincarnated soul is necessarily accompanied by a demon, a "dispenser spirit". Today we would probably call such a spirit a protecting or guardian angel. This demon is our connection with our superior self, who in turn connects us with the higher forces of the Universe. The reason for the intervention of such a demon is something unavoidable, since only such a spirit can form the link between our inferior and superior self.

What is asked from the reincarnated souls to achieve is the integrated function of the *trimereia* of the *inferior* self, because the *trimereia* of the superior self is considered complete from the beginning, since only the inferior self has fallen (see Chapter 3).

The demon who accompanies our soul is responsible for the function of our reincarnation. This is our counsellor and our punisher. Depending on the way of life we choose, the demon becomes either a malevolent or a benevolent spirit and will eventually put an end to our life, but is not the one who will take this decision.

In other words, if the way we live is dictated by the application of virtues that result in acting good and doing good to as many persons as we can, then our demon will function as a benevolent spirit and will reward us with a happy life (the Greek word *eudaemon* = happy comes from the combination of the words *eu* = good, and *daemon*), which will most probably end with a calm and painless death. But if our way of life does not follow the above principles, then our demon will punish us by functioning as a malevolent spirit in order to teach us the appropriate lesson, which we apparently need so that we will be forced to change our mind; for, if we do not, our future can be painful, probably in the Tartarus as in the case of Ardiaeus the tyrant. Of course, such an outcome would signify the total failure of our current reincarnation.

Therefore, it should be understood that our demon is the entity who determines important details of our life. According to this line of thought, the ageing process and death are consequences of not following the proper evolution that would be brought about by the *technosis* of our mind: The reason we eventually die is because we never learn any piece of this mystic knowledge, since during our whole adult life we remain unreceptive of learning; as a result, our demon is finally forced to take our life, when it is decided that the suitable time has come.

Πρῶτος δ' ὁ λαχὼν πρῶτος αἰρείσθω βίον ᾧ συνέσται ἐξ ἀνάγκης.

4. Let the [soul] to whom falls the first lot first select a life to be linked with, out of necessity.

....

The soul chosen first will select the particular human body with which it will necessarily coexist. In an alternative, quite different interpretation of this passage, if the soul manages to acquire a benevolent demon as a companion for the impending reincarnation, this spirit will free that life from the fatal consequence of the death described in the previous terms.

This is the fourth term of the "contract" and can be viewed as the "centre of gravity" of all seven terms. The logic of the whole contract and of the reincarnation revolves around its understanding.

In what follows, Plato describes how our soul could fall in the category described by the fourth term.

_____

Ἀρετὴ δὲ ἀδέσποτον,...

5. Virtue has no master over it.

....

Virtue is not the property of anybody; however, if the souls are accompanied by a benevolent demon, then they can conquer virtue. The word *adespoton* can also mean the one who does not act like a master, one who is not imposed on anyone, so that he or she is able to control his or her selfishness. Thus, it can be said that the basic prerequisite for the appearance and escorting by a benevolent demon is the lack of selfishness from our soul.

The Greek word *egoismos*, which means egoism, selfishness, is especially revealing, as it contains an anagram of the Greek word misos, which means "half" and also "hatred"! In other words, selfishness is what keeps our true self "half", by keeping our superior and inferior selves separated, and then hatred appears in our behaviour.

One of the worst consequences of selfishness is fanaticism. Fanaticism is probably the worst state that could be experienced by a soul; it could eventually lead souls to the path followed by the soul of Ardiaeus the tyrant and throw them into the Tartarus. This fact, too, is reflected in an anagram in the Greek language, which explains the results of fanaticism, a state that can be viewed as an expression of extreme selfishness: FANATISMOS = AFAN(T)ISMOS, that is FANATICISM = extermination.

... ἣν τιμῶν καὶ ἀτιμάζων πλέον καὶ ἔλαττον αὐτῆς ἕκαστος ἕξει.

6. Each will have more or less of virtue as he honours or dishonours it.

In the previous context, virtue is the inverse of selfishness: more virtue means less selfishness and vice-versa. However, even a small quantity of selfish behaviour suffices for the failure of our attempt to reach immortality in this world. Therefore, the reincarnated souls have two alternatives: Either to completely control their selfishness and break the fatal (i.e. determined by the Fates) cycle of reincarnations, or to function more or less selfishly and thus fail to achieve immortality.

Αἰτία ἑλομένου: θεὸς ἀναίτιος.»

7. The blame belongs to the one who chooses; God is blameless."

What Plato wants to stress here is that the souls are the sole responsible parts for the behaviour of the demon who will accompany each one of them; the reason for their punishment will be the choices they will make during their lives. So they should not blame any god as being responsible for their failure.

The speech of the soul on the elevated podium ends in a culmination: the declaration of the most important issue pertaining to the life of any human being.

Each soul must announce that we ourselves are the ones who determine our fate, depending on our deeds. We are the ones who must study and decide upon the way that will allow us to conquer immortality!

As a conclusion, seven important terms are communicated to the reader, so that he or she will be informed about what determines the whole path of the human soul's reincarnation. However, the most important of all is to understand that as humans we possess a great weapon called Free Will, which must manage to exploit, for only in such a case we will be able to achieve our personal evolution and will not remain a member of a herd of animals that follow, almost by definition, a common, "group evolution".

What is actually meant by "signing" the above "contract" is that the souls, each one separately, should strive at any cost to find a way to escape from the herd to which we belong and to make the impossible possible in order to achieve our personal (and thus "responsible") evolution.

This is the great secret of our life and of the "contract" we have "signed" as incorporeal souls — but we have forgotten that we have, as humans.

The result of not keeping the terms of the contract is the punishment of the embodied soul with death, to which our demon is forced to lead us, because of the law of necessity-entropy.

It would not be extravagant to say that in this "contract" is contained, according to Plato, the essence of philosophy and the meaning of the human life.

Therefore, as a conclusion, it can be said that Plato urges his readers to understand this great truth and to study philosophy as seriously as they can. In other words, the reader should try at any cost to fulfil all seven "contract terms" in order to attain immortality, and not be limited in acknowledging only the first term, as is usually the case, because in such an instance we are led to certain death.

Chapter 11
THE PROCESS OF SELECTING
THE NEXT REINCARNATION

Ταῦτα εἰπόντα ῥῖψαι ἐπὶ πάντας τοὺς κλήρους, τὸν δὲ παρ' αὐτὸν πεσόντα ἕκαστον ἀναιρεῖσθαι πλὴν οὗ, ἃ δὲ οὐκ ἐᾶν: τῷ δὲ ἀνελομένῳ δῆλον εἶναι ὁπόστος εἰλήχει. [618a] μετὰ δὲ τοῦτο αὖθις τὰ τῶν βίων παραδείγματα εἰς τὸ πρόσθεν σφῶν θεῖναι ἐπὶ τὴν γῆν, πολὺ πλείω τῶν παρόντων. εἶναι δὲ παντοδαπά: ζῴων τε γὰρ πάντων βίους καὶ δὴ καὶ τοὺς ἀνθρωπίνους ἅπαντας. τυραννίδας τε γὰρ ἐν αὑτοῖς εἶναι, τὰς μὲν διατελεῖς, τὰς δὲ καὶ μεταξὺ διαφθειρομένας καὶ εἰς πενίας τε καὶ φυγὰς καὶ εἰς πτωχείας τελευτώσας: εἶναι δὲ καὶ δοκίμων ἀνδρῶν βίους, τοὺς μὲν ἐπὶ εἴδεσιν καὶ κατὰ κάλλη καὶ τὴν ἄλλην ἰσχὺν [618b] τε καὶ ἀγωνίαν, τοὺς δ' ἐπὶ γένεσιν καὶ προγόνων ἀρεταῖς, καὶ ἀδοκίμων κατὰ ταῦτα, ὡσαύτως δὲ καὶ γυναικῶν. ψυχῆς δὲ τάξιν οὐκ ἐνεῖναι διὰ τὸ ἀναγκαίως ἔχειν ἄλλον ἑλομένην βίον ἀλλοίαν γίγνεσθαι: τὰ δ' ἄλλα ἀλλήλοις τε καὶ πλούτοις καὶ πενίαις, τὰ δὲ νόσοις, τὰ δ' ὑγιείαις μεμεῖχθαι, τὰ δὲ καὶ μεσοῦν τούτων.

Ταῦτα εἰπόντα ῥῖψαι ἐπὶ πάντας τοὺς κλήρους,...

After these had been said, he (the prophet) flung the lots out among them all,...

... δι' τὸν δὲ παρ' αὐτὸν πεσόντα ἕκαστον ἀναιρεῖσθαι πλὴν οὗ, ἓ δὲ οὐκ ἐᾶν,...

... and each [soul] took up the lot that fell by the side of each [soul], except their own [lot]; that they did not permit.

After Er has mentioned the terms of the "incarnation contract", he now proceeds to explain the manner in which each soul can exert its right to choose the lot (i.e. the roles that soul would be able to assume as an embodied entity). It is important at this point to repeat that to each lot corresponds one demon, which the soul has no right to reject; for it is not allowed to the inferior self to refuse the escort of the demon. This tiny word in the ancient text, e, can indeed be interpreted to mean our inferior self.

... τῷ δὲ ἀνελομένῳ δῆλον εἶναι ὁπόστος εἰλήχει.

And each soul that took up a lot saw plainly what number had been drawn.

As far as the selection of the demon who accompanies each lot is concerned, it is evident that whatever his quality is on the topic of virtue, the soul is obliged to accept his presence, regardless of being displeased with it. The demon accompanies the soul from the moment the latter reads the number on the lot, being still outside of a body.

The reason that the souls must not feel disgruntled if they realise that their demon is not as good as expected is that in the "contract" they signed, they accepted that they must "play their role" as humans in such a way that they will force their demon to function as a benevolent one. The performance of the souls should be such that it will not provoke their demon to punish them, but instead it will support and reward them. This could be achieved only with the development and the training of each soul's Free Will.

Μετὰ δὲ τοῦτο αὖθις τὰ τῶν βίων παραδείγματα εἰς τὸ πρόσθεν σφῶν θεῖναι ἐπὶ τὴν γῆν,...

And after this again he promptly placed the patterns of lives before them on the ground,...

... πολὺ πλείω τῶν παρόντων.

... and these were far more numerous than the souls.

Immediately after the choosing of the lots, the content of each one is revealed; it pertains to specific roles or human lives, one of which each soul must select, in order to be embodied in the respective human body in the next reincarnation on Earth. Since there are many more lots than souls, this means that actually the souls could choose their demon: If the souls want to satisfy their real needs, then they can select a lot accompanied by a benevolent demon;

197

however, such a lot will obviously put the soul into a difficult role, which would require a great effort on the soul's part in order to meet its standards.

What we humans have learned from our society, the prevailing "normal" view, is to select always a life during which we will "have a good time". In accordance with this stance, it would be reasonable for the Platonic souls to want to choose apparently pleasant roles, which, however, are obviously accompanied by malevolent demons.

The reason the number of lots, and hence of the demons, is much greater than the number of the assembled souls is that the souls, according to the third term, must have the right to choose a benevolent demon.

An additional right of the souls is that of the detailed and deep examination of their next reincarnation. If the particular lot received by a given soul is examined in detail and is rejected, then the soul has the right to exchange it with another lot. Yet, although they have been clearly given this right, the souls usually do not make use of it, because most probably they still function thoughtlessly and, as it seems, they are too anxious to be reincarnated.

Εἶναι δὲ παντοδαπά:

The content of these lots was of every possible variety:

... ζώων τε γὰρ πάντων βίους καὶ δὴ καὶ τοὺς ἀνθρωπίνους ἅπαντας.

... there were lives of all kinds of animals and all sorts of human lives.

According to Plato, there were even choices of roles that would lead to the transmigration of the soul to some animal. In the context of Ancient Greek philosophy, the term "metempsychosis" is preferably used when we include reincarnations of souls to both animals and humans. The theory of transmigration of human souls to animals and of animal souls to humans is the necessary and rational complement to the reincarnation law. Based on this belief, which is common in Hinduism, the great increase of the human world population can be explained, since apparently many animals can have after their death their souls transmigrate to newborn humans.

Of course, it should be considered reasonable that in their first metempsychosis to human bodies these former animal souls should belong to the first Aristotelian level of human evolution, namely the humanoid or "two-legged creature" or "slave".

Τυραννίδας τε γὰρ ἐν αὑτοῖς εἶναι,...

There were lives of tyrants among them,...

The notion of tyrant here corresponds to the modern notion of any person that has political power.

... τὰς μὲν διατελεῖς,...

199

some uninterrupted till the end,...

... τὰς δὲ καὶ μεταξὺ διαφθειρομένας καὶ εἰς πενίας τε καὶ φυγὰς καὶ εἰς πτωχείας τελευτώσας.

... and others destroyed midway and resulting in penuries and exiles and poverty;...

This passage could be taken to mean that, although certain souls perform their role of tyrant in the same way throughout their lives, there are some other souls that freely choose to change their character of the role and perform it in a way that rejects the element of power and leads to a life of poverty and/or in exile. Thus, we conclude that, while a given soul had received a lot of a tyrant (most probably accompanied by a malevolent demon), that soul managed to understand through the adequate development of Free Will that this role is not conducive to evolution and decided to radically change its interpretation, up to the point the malevolent demon was transformed into a benevolent one. In other words, that particular soul fulfilled the fourth term of the "contract"!

We should understand that the reason Plato writes about this impressive alternative is in order for the readers to adopt it in case they examine their role in life and realise that it is not helpful in the evolution of their soul.

Thus, if we want to be worthy of the title of human, we have to examine, through the knowledge of the self, the performance of our role; if that performance does not satisfy us, then we should make all the necessary improvisations, using our Free Will, in order to convert the role into a helpful one for our soul's evolution.

How different would our life be if we realised this inherent possibility and decided to keep the fourth term of the reincarnation "contract"?

... εἶναι δὲ καὶ δοκίμων ἀνδρῶν βίους,...

... and there were also other lives of men famous,...

... τοὺς μὲν ἐπὶ εἴδεσιν καὶ κατὰ κάλλη...

... for their external appearance and beauty,...

....

Still, by making use of their Free Will, these men can also decide that it would be preferable to exchange their fame with anonymity.

... καὶ τὴν ἄλλην ἰσχύν τε καὶ ἀγωνίαν, τοὺς δ᾽ ἐπὶ γένεσιν καὶ προγόνων ἀρεταῖς,...

... and for their prowess and noble blood, and for the virtues of their ancestors,...

... καὶ ἀδοκίμων κατὰ ταῦτα,...

... and others of ill repute in the same things,...

Here Plato hints at the well-known fact that some people are famous because they have struggled themselves a lot to ascend the social ladder and to attain their goals, rising from anonymity to fame, while others, being famous by birth, end up in living an insignificant life, probably by choice.

At this point we could compare with the famous phrase of Epicurus lathe biosas = "live in obscurity", which supports the view that a life considered by most people insignificant could be much more constructive in terms of soul evolution than the life of a famous person, which is full of excitement and disturbance of mind, and does not lead to the evolution of the soul.

In the case of the Myth of Er, Alcinous is the famous king whose life does not allow the evolution of his soul, while the *Alkimos* Er is the insignificant soldier who nobody knows, yet eventually he manages to evolve his soul.

... ὡσαύτως δὲ καὶ γυναικῶν.

... and similarly of women.

Ψυχῆς δὲ τάξιν οὐκ ἐνεῖναι διὰ τὸ ἀναγκαίως ἔχειν ἄλλον ἐλομένην βίον ἀλλοίαν γίγνεσθαι:...

However, there was no determination of the quality of soul, because the choice of a different life inevitably determines a different character;...

All the previous roles, according to Plato, can be equally well assigned to male and female bodies. There are no specific limitations regarding the improvisations in the role performance made by a soul; this means that, whatever role (character) the soul chooses, the possibility to evolve is still present.

This means that in our life there is a great necessity; since we are necessarily called to impersonate roles, this means that all persons during their embodied lives operate like actors and actresses.

The aim of an actor is to use all his abilities during his performance in order to impersonate his role in the best possible way, so that he will offer the best example of what the life of the character he impersonates was like. This is what a free interpretation of the etymology of the Greek word *ethopoios* (= actor) means: the one who sets an example, a habit (*ethos*). Evidently, for being able to achieve this, a good actor should not impersonate his character by merely reading his lines, nor spend his abilities for an indifferent and skin-deep impersonation. Instead, he must penetrate at any cost to the deeper essence of his role and he must improvise at the points he feels they should be modified.

This is exactly the case of the tyrants mentioned previously, whose souls decided to play their roles by following a different path, which would be better for their own evolution. Still, in order to gain the required strength that will allow them to handle such a difficult improvisation, they must cultivate their *ethos*, which also means "moral strength". This cultivation is the only way to train their Free

Will, with which we are all endowed.

This is the central and great message Plato attempts to communicate to his readers, a truth which apparently we are yet to realise. We have been told that, as humans, we are equipped with the faculty of the Free Will. However, we have not understood that, if we have not first cultivated our moral strength, which is probably the basic topic in moral philosophy, the capability for Free Will loses all its value and is useless. In order to manage to use successfully our Free Will and to operate it in the right way, we have as a prerequisite to be educated in three basic fields according to the ancient Greek thought: *catharsis* (cleansing), initiation, and philosophy.

Any person who lives in the society is subjected every day to a continuous "brainwashing" towards the direction of the society's prevailing views; therefore, his or her will is not truly "free", as he or she is continuously led, or even misled, to act according to the collective prevailing "will" of the specific society. Thus, as long as we live inside a human society, we end up exerting a "Directed Will" while believing that our acts and decisions are determined by our own will; unfortunately, they express the will of other people. And for the vast majority of humans it is extremely difficult to understand that the only thing they do by using their supposedly Free Will is to function as blind carriers of the orders of those who have the power to shape the public opinion.

The basic educational purpose of a good theatrical play is exactly to force its audience to understand the objective reality through the *catharsis* it causes to them; in this way, it leads them to use correctly their own Free Will.

... τὰ δ' ἄλλα ἀλλήλοις τε καὶ πλούτοις καὶ πενίαις,...

as for all other things, however, they were mixed with one another and with wealth and poverty,...

The above passage can be interpreted to mean that certain souls, wishing to cultivate their strength, choose to play roles that alternate between two opposite states, for example between a rich and a poor way of living. In other words, these souls select a life in which they will experience great and intense contrasts.

Indeed, we should accept that the greater strengthening of a soul could be achieved when it is proved in practice that this soul can survive with equal ease under conditions of both wealth and poverty.

... τὰ δὲ νόσοις, τὰ δ' ὑγιείαις μεμεῖχθαι,...

... and with sickness and health,...

... τὰ δὲ καὶ μεσοῦν τούτων.

... and the intermediate conditions.

Similarly, we can assume from the above that there are some other souls who choose for their strengthening to perform roles that alternate between sickness and health; and finally, that there are still other souls who choose to be reincarnated to lives that will not experience such bipolar alternations.

Presumably, the latter souls are the most advanced, as they have most probably passed through all these extreme states during previous reincarnations and now are closer to intermediate and equilibrated states. In their case it is easier to improvise in the performance of their role, since they will not have to move between extreme situations.

At this point, we could understand completely the metaphor of the function of the eight Sirens and the three Fates, if we assume that the above performance of a life's role is related to the performance of a musical composition.

The Sirens emit musical notes that determine the melody and the tempo of such a composition.

The Fates express the three musical clefs, which determine the pitch of the "voice" of the Sirens. That is, whether their melody will be heard in a soprano's high pitch (that represents the present time), in a mezzo-soprano's middle pitch (representing the future), or in a contralto's low pitch (representing the past).

As long as a soul remains unevolved, that soul is represented by the low pitch and lives in the past, while a soul who becomes more cultivated is led through the present towards the future. Thus, the three clefs correspond to the present, the past and the future.

In the context of this metaphor, the music of Apollo's lyre, which had seven strings, is connected with the function of our soul. Hence, the combination of the Sirens and the Fates could produce a perfect musical composition, which has the power to influence a soul and thus to contribute to that soul's evolution. On the contrary, an inadequate combination could lead our soul to a disaster.

This is probably the reason that the knowledge of music and musical education were so important to the Greeks, the music being one of the main courses taught to a child.

As it has been mentioned in Chapter 9, the three Fates (Moirai) control our life and one of them has a priority over it.

As we are able to surmise from what has been said about the roles and the Free Will, we can decide about how we want to perform our role by using our Free Will; we just have to understand that we can modify the "lines of the play", like a good actor can improvise.

We have exactly the same capability when we face a philosophical ancient text. As we have ascertained many times, the ancient texts are written in such a way that not only they are undogmatic, but they call openly for several different levels of interpretation.

If we translate an ancient text *verbatim*, we will produce a very inadequate translation, exactly as if we just recited our role in a theatrical play word-by-word, in which case we would give a very bad performance.

This means that the ancient texts can be compared to lots from the knees of Lachesis, which scholars and interested readers alike are called to decipher and to try to benefit from them as much as possible. The difficulty in understanding the deeper meaning of these texts is not because of lack of knowledge of how to translate them, but rather because of lack of knowledge of how to decode them. Metaphorically, in order to do that we would use the two other "clefs", which would allow us to comprehend what these texts would have to say to us about the present and even more what they would have to say about the future.

Another related aspect of several ancient Greek texts we call "philosophical" is their sacred nature, which calls for their comparison with the sibyllic manner of phrasing of the holy prophetic responses of Apollo in Delphi

A reason why many Greek texts are as ambiguous as the famous Delphic oracles is that they do not dogmatize. Instead, the permit the reader, even 2,500 years later, to choose freely the personal interpretation he or she wants to assign to them, depending on the evolution of his or her soul.

In this sense, every ancient Greek text is a lot calling for an adequate interpretation, as in the case of Er, i.e. like h-ER-oes capable of applying their own Free Will.

Chapter 12
THE GRANDEUR OF THE FREE WILL
and its key contribution
to spiritual upgrade

Ἔνθα δή, ὡς ἔοικεν, ὦ φίλε Γλαύκων, ὁ πᾶς κίνδυνος ἀνθρώπῳ, καὶ διὰ ταῦτα μάλιστα [618c] ἐπιμελητέον ὅπως ἕκαστος
ἡμῶν τῶν ἄλλων μαθημάτων ἀμελήσας τούτου τοῦ μαθήματος καὶ ζητητὴς καὶ μαθητὴς ἔσται, ἐάν ποθεν οἷός τ᾽ ᾖ μαθεῖν καὶ ἐξευρεῖν τίς αὐτὸν ποιήσει δυνατὸν καὶ ἐπιστήμονα,
βίον καὶ χρηστὸν καὶ πονηρὸν διαγιγνώσκοντα, τὸν βελτίω
ἐκ τῶν δυνατῶν ἀεὶ πανταχοῦ αἱρεῖσθαι· ἀναλογιζόμενον
πάντα τὰ νυνδὴ ῥηθέντα καὶ συντιθέμενα ἀλλήλοις καὶ διαιρούμενα πρὸς ἀρετὴν βίου πῶς ἔχει, εἰδέναι τί κάλλος πενίᾳ
ἢ πλούτῳ κραθὲν καὶ [618d] μετὰ ποίας τινὸς ψυχῆς ἕξεως
κακὸν ἢ ἀγαθὸν ἐργάζεται, καὶ τί εὐγένειαι καὶ δυσγένειαι
καὶ ἰδιωτεῖαι καὶ ἀρχαὶ καὶ ἰσχύες καὶ ἀσθένειαι καὶ εὐμαθίαι
καὶ δυσμαθίαι καὶ πάντα τὰ τοιαῦτα τῶν φύσει περὶ ψυχὴν
ὄντων καὶ τῶν ἐπικτήτων τί συγκεραννύμενα πρὸς ἄλληλα
ἐργάζεται, ὥστε ἐξ ἁπάντων αὐτῶν δυνατὸν εἶναι συλλογισάμενον αἱρεῖσθαι, πρὸς τὴν τῆς ψυχῆς φύσιν ἀποβλέποντα,
τόν τε χείρω καὶ τὸν ἀμείνω [618e] βίον, χείρω μὲν καλοῦντα
ὃς αὐτὴν ἐκεῖσε ἄξει, εἰς τὸ ἀδικωτέραν γίγνεσθαι, ἀμείνω δὲ

ὅστις είς τὸ δικαιοτέραν.

Ἔνθα δή, ὡς ἔοικεν, ὦ φίλε Γλαύκων, ὁ πᾶς κίνδυνος ἀνθρώπῳ,...

And there, dear Glaucon, it appears, lies the supreme danger for a human,...

In one sense, the greatest danger Plato refers to here is for us to end up being bad actors! Indeed, a bad interpretation of the role we perform as reincarnated souls can become very dangerous for the particular person.

We should eventually understand that the role assigned by Lachesis to a soul is not actually that important. The roles differ in their difficulty of performance, but the weight of a role falls on the performance delivered by the specific actor or actress. It is here that the issue of the Free Will enters, because if we perform our role verbatim our performance will be truly very bad and finally dangerous. If, on the contrary, we improvise as expert actors do, entering under the skin of the role and at the same time expressing our individual idiosyncrasy, then we can greatly improve the message the role communicates and modify its given characteristics.

Such an example is given by the tyrants of the previous chapter, who stopped exerting arbitrary and repressive power upon their subjects and instead they concentrated on evolving their souls. This example proves that even the worst role, if played with the suitable improvisations, ceases to be hazardous to the soul and can become beneficial. On the contrary, a bad execution of a good role could seriously damage the soul evolution of the "actor".

At the end of the line, what we are asked to do is to become competent actors and to perform our role by employing the moral virtues, in case of course we have cultivated them before.

This is the reason that in ancient Greece the role of actor was assumed by those who had attained épopteia, the initiated ones of the Eleusinian Mysteries, who were presumably initiated in the field of moral virtues.

Therefore, we should not limit ourselves to the cultivation of the intellectual virtues only, as king Alcinous did, who had cultivated these virtues to the highest degree, but he had not cultivated the moral virtues and hence he was a "bad actor": He didn't know how to improvise, because he functioned like a modern scientist not interested in moral values, who thinks that his intellectual powers are enough for him to be compared even with God himself.

Improvisation gives us the opportunity to demonstrate if and to what extent we have assimilate and practice the moral values. Otherwise, if we execute the "screenplay" of our life by just reciting its words, we will never operate our Free Will. In such a case our actions will be no different from the programmed function of a robot that is equipped with a computer.

As a conclusion, we should understand the fact that in our life we have two choices: either to perform our role mechanically, functioning as robots and ancient slaves, or to improvise during its performance. In the first case, we cannot enter the "paradise" and we end up condemned to live chained inside Plato's Cave (the famous allegory described earlier in the *Republic,* 514a–520a), following blindly the plans of those in power. In the second case, and if we improvise based on the moral values, we will be able to break our bondage and to function as real humans. This is the path to which we are led when we study Greek philosophy.

... καὶ διὰ ταῦτα μάλιστα ἐπιμελητέον ὅπως ἕκαστος ἡμῶν τῶν ἄλλων μαθημάτων ἀμελήσας τούτου τοῦ μαθήματος καὶ ζητητὴς καὶ μαθητὴς ἔσται,...

... and above all this is the reason why it should be our main care that each of us, neglecting all other studies, should seek after and learn the following thing:...

... ἐάν ποθεν οἷός τ' ᾖ μαθεῖν καὶ ἐξευρεῖν τίς αὐτὸν ποιήσει δυνατὸν καὶ ἐπιστήμονα,...

... if in any way he may be able to learn of and discover the one who will make him strong enough and knowledgeable...

....

What "each of us" should seek is how to be protected from dangers arising from an inadequate interpretation of his or her role. This is the single most important parameter we should pay attention to, according to Plato. The souls who will manage to perform their role correctly will acquire great strength and lots of knowledge, enough to evolve them into real "scientists" (*epistemones*) in the Platonic sense; that is, persons who, in parallel with the acquisition of knowledge, also cultivate the tremendous powers of their souls, in other words the moral virtues that will assist them to perform much better in their roles and evolve their souls.

Unfortunately, most "scientists" in our days either ignore or do not assign any value to the moral dimension of the evolution of their soul, which, as we have seen, could lessen the burden of their karmic debt.

While Socrates teaches the intellectual virtues with his dialectical method, he also urges his students to attend the Eleusinian Mysteries, where an initiation to the moral values takes place. This initiation was known as "Descent to Hades" and this is exactly the theme of the Myth of Er; thus, it can be said that this Myth introduces us to the Eleusinian initiation. Moreover, the Socratic dialectic itself serves also the same need, being the unique method in the whole ancient world that could awaken the Free Will, which is inherent in embryonic state inside us, in the *thymetikon* or thymoid part of our soul, and must be reborn; Socrates possesses the "midwifery" (*maieutics*) method that will extract it from that state and will transfer it in a newborn form.

... βίον καὶ χρηστὸν καὶ πονηρὸν διαγιγνώσκοντα,...

... to distinguish the life that is good from that which is bad, ...

... τὸν βελτίω ἐκ τῶν δυνατῶν ἀεὶ πανταχοῦ αἱρεῖσθαι:...

... and always and everywhere to choose the best that the conditions allow;...

The knowledgeable souls will know which should be the correct way to perform their role, which corresponds to human act-ors; on the other side, they will know that a bad performance will relegate them to the realm of the dangerous beasts.

Moreover, the souls should realise that they have to perform their role in the best possible manner in the whole of their reincarnated lives and under any circumstances.

The paradigm of the perfect actor is given for the ancient Greek reader of Plato by Dionysus, who introduced for the first time the mystic function of theatre. Of course, theatre nowadays, in its present form, has no mystical character whatsoever and hence it is unable to carry out its ancient Greek function, which was to elevate the spectators from the level of "humanoid" to the level of human.

... ἀναλογιζόμενον πάντα τὰ νυνδὴ ῥηθέντα καὶ συντιθέμενα ἀλλήλοις καὶ διαιρούμενα πρὸς ἀρετὴν βίου πῶς ἔχει,...

... and, considering all the things of which we have spoken and estimating the effect on the virtue of his life of their mutual concurrence or their separate occurrence,...

... εἰδέναι τί κάλλος πενίᾳ ἢ πλούτῳ κραθὲν καὶ μετὰ ποίας τινὸς ψυχῆς ἕξεως κακὸν ἢ ἀγαθὸν ἐργάζεται,...

... knowing, that is, how beauty combined with poverty or wealth and with what habit of soul functions for good or for evil,...

Thus, if some person takes into account the previous parts of the Myth of Er and, considering the types of life depending on their characteristics, makes a synthesis, and proceeds, moreover, to analyse the manner of application of all the above, then the soul of that person will manage, through the operation of the Free Will, to live a truly virtuous life (i.e. one that will emphasise the moral virtues).

Under these prerequisites, such persons could withstand even the most difficult life conditions and to understand, for example, how much beauty could accompany poverty and, on the other hand, how much beauty could be hidden under the right handling of wealth. They could also understand how to follow a virtuous or a wicked life, according to the extent they have been addicted to the application of the moral virtues. Because the Eleusinian initiation does not teach the moral virtues; it rather *addicts* us to them.

... καὶ τί εὐγένειαι καὶ δυσγένειαι καὶ ἰδιωτεῖαι...

... and what are the effects of high and low birth and private standing...

215

The above passage can also be interpreted to mean that the kind of performance of a role can finally lead the soul to express a polite or an impolite behaviour. The most important issue here is how humans will understand the reason their souls must avoid behaving with selfishness. Egoism comes in when we perform our role *verbatim*. The selfish persons have not the opportunity to express their Free Will in any way, so they cannot evolve their souls and as a consequence they will live a "useless", senseless and even dangerous life.

All humanoids or "slaves" function in a purely selfish way, for egoism is primarily contained in the instinct of self-preservation. This is a characteristic indispensable and absolutely useful for the animals, but it certainly poses obstacles to those human souls that want to evolve. Selfishness probably favors group evolution, however it hinders personal evolution.

... καὶ ἀρχαὶ καὶ ἰσχύες καὶ ἀσθένειαι...

...and office and strength and weakness...

... καὶ εὐμαθίαι καὶ δυσμαθίαι...

... and aptitude for learning and difficulties in learning...

... καὶ πάντα τὰ τοιαῦτα τῶν φύσει περὶ ψυχὴν ὄντων καὶ τῶν ἐπικτήτων τί συγκεραννύμενα πρὸς ἄλληλα ἐργάζεται,...

... and all similar natural and acquired properties of the soul, when mixed and combined with one another,...

... ὥστε ἐξ ἁπάντων αὐτῶν δυνατὸν εἶναι συλλογισά-μενον αἱρεῖσθαι,...

... so that with consideration of all these things he will be able to make a thoughtful choice,...

... πρὸς τὴν τῆς ψυχῆς φύσιν ἀποβλέποντα, τόν τε χείρω καὶ τὸν ἀμείνω βίον,...

... having in mind the nature of the soul, between the worse and the better life,...

... χείρω μὲν καλοῦντα ὃς αὐτὴν ἐκεῖσε ἄξει, εἰς τὸ ἀδικωτέραν γίγνεσθαι,...

..., calling worse the life that will tend to make [the soul] more unjust...

... ἀμείνω δὲ ὅστις εἰς τὸ δικαιοτέραν.

... and better that which will make [the soul] more just.

So the knowledgeable humans will manage to comprehend the principles that should govern their soul in order to have a strong and healthy soul, and not a weak one.

They will also learn under which circumstances will have

the opportunity to be taught and, on the other hand, which bad habits will render them unreceptive of learning.

At a subsequent stage, these humans should combine all the good elements that pre-exist in their souls, their natural talents, with the acquired experiences from the present reincarnation, and to juxtapose them to the negative elements in order to have a complete picture of their inner world. Then they will be able to achieve the ideal synthesis that will justify their reincarnation.

In such a case, they would lead their soul to evolution, since that soul will be in a position to know which is the worst and which is the best way of function of the Free Will: The worst way we could perform our role would be to behave unjustly; this behaviour would rescind Free Will and would lead us to compromise the evolution of our soul. On the contrary, the best way to perform our role should aim at a behaviour that would be more and more just, so that our soul would be led towards a continuous spiritual upgrading.

Chapter 13
GUIDELINES TO TRAVELLERS

Τὰ δὲ ἄλλα πάντα χαίρειν ἐάσει: ἑωράκαμεν γὰρ ὅτι ζῶντί τε καὶ τελευτήσαντι αὕτη κρατίστη αἵρεσις. ἀδαμαντίνως δὴ [619a] δεῖ ταύτην τὴν δόξαν ἔχοντα εἰς Ἅιδου ἰέναι, ὅπως ἂν ᾖ καὶ ἐκεῖ ἀνέκπληκτος ὑπὸ πλούτων τε καὶ τῶν τοιούτων κακῶν, καὶ μὴ ἐμπεσὼν εἰς τυραννίδας καὶ ἄλλας τοιαύτας πράξεις πολλὰ μὲν ἐργάσηται καὶ ἀνήκεστα κακά, ἔτι δὲ αὐτὸς μείζω πάθῃ, ἀλλὰ γνῷ τὸν μέσον ἀεὶ τῶν τοιούτων βίον αἱρεῖσθαι καὶ φεύγειν τὰ ὑπερβάλλοντα ἑκατέρωσε καὶ ἐν τῷδε τῷ βίῳ κατὰ τὸ δυνατὸν καὶ ἐν παντὶ τῷ ἔπειτα: οὕτω γὰρ [619b] εὐδαιμονέστατος γίγνεται ἄνθρωπος. Καὶ δὴ οὖν καὶ τότε ὁ ἐκεῖθεν ἄγγελος ἤγγελλε τὸν μὲν προφήτην οὕτως εἰπεῖν: «καὶ τελευταίῳ ἐπιόντι, ξὺν νῷ ἑλομένῳ, συντόνως ζῶντι κεῖται βίος ἀγαπητός, οὐ κακός. μήτε ὁ ἄρχων αἱρέσεως ἀμελείτω μήτε ὁ τελευτῶν ἀθυμείτω.»

Τὰ δὲ ἄλλα πάντα χαίρειν ἐάσει:...

But he will happily dismiss all other alternatives;...

Socrates says here effectively that he would be very happy if all humans would neglect all other intellectual or spiritual pursuits in favour of the one they would consider the most important: the development of their Free Will and hence the adequate performance of their role.

Thus we realise that nothing else matters more for Socrates than a honest occupation with philosophy, with the purpose of developing one's Free Will. It follows that the content of the Myth of Er pertains to the highest philosophical pursuit; any other pursuit is considered secondary. This effort can be also considered as the distilled essence of the Socratic dialectic method, that is to lead the soul to the direction of developing Free Will and to create a spiritual mixture consisting of the elements of our character with the aim of reducing our mistakes and increasing our virtues.

... ἑωράκαμεν γὰρ ὅτι ζῶντί τε καὶ τελευτήσαντι αὕτη κρατίστη αἵρεσις.

... because we have understood that this is the best choice for both the living and the dead.

....

The significance of the previous effort lies in the fact that its pertains to the evolution of both the embodied soul and the soul in heavens. Only a person who functions properly a truly Free Will can achieve the integrated development of his or her soul. Such souls know what to do both when they are embodied and when they are free.

Ἀδαμαντίνως δὴ δεῖ ταύτην τὴν δόξαν ἔχοντα εἰς Ἅιδου ἰέναι,...

One must take with him to Hades an unyielding faith in this,...

... ὅπως ἂν ἦ καὶ ἐκεῖ ἀνέκπληκτος ὑπὸ πλούτων τε καὶ τῶν τοιούτων κακῶν,...

... so that even there he would be undazzled by riches and similar negative distractions,...

Any person who possesses this extremely valuable knowledge about the proper function of the Free Will must keep it when the time of death comes and descends to the kingdom of the dead. For, if we are equipped with this knowledge, then we will be able to remain calm and fearless. The reader will probably recall at this point the way Socrates remained calm and fearless when he drank the poison hemlock.

As a result, such souls will avoid in their next reincarnation roles closely connected either to material wealth or to other materialistic pleasures, which could easily harm them. Proceeding in this line of thought, in connection with the previous chapters, these souls will be able during the time of the lot choice to prefer the best life roles, selecting them among a multitude of bad ones, because they will retain the ability of Free Will in Hades and hence they are in a position to choose the lives they know that can offer them the best opportunities for good role performance and evolution.

... καὶ μὴ ἐμπεσὼν εἰς τυραννίδας καὶ ἄλλας τοιαύτας πράξεις πολλὰ μὲν ἐργάσηται καὶ ἀνήκεστα κακά,...

... and he would not fall into tyrannies and similar activities and thus perpetrate many and incurable crimes,...

The knowledgeable souls will not choose roles of persons who have political power, such as tyrants, because roles of that kind could cause to them significant damages, serious enough to send them to the Tartarus.

The purpose of a reincarnation must be the evolution of the soul and not the enjoyment of power on Earth, which, as it can be observed, can become very dangerous.

... ἔτι δὲ αὐτὸς μείζω πάθῃ,...

... and suffer still greater ordeals himself,...

... ἀλλὰ γνῷ τὸν μέσον ἀεὶ τῶν τοιούτων βίον αἱρεῖσθαι...

.. but instead he would know how always to select among such possibilities the "average" life...

... καὶ φεύγειν τὰ ὑπερβάλλοντα ἑκατέρωσε καὶ ἐν τῷδε τῷ βίῳ κατὰ τὸ δυνατὸν καὶ ἐν παντὶ τῷ ἔπειτα:...

... and to avoid the excess in either direction, both in this earthly life as far as possible and in all the lives to come;...

In other words, if a given soul manages to live in a fair, legitimate, equilibrated and moral way its present life, a way which exercises the virtues and lies close to the middle (*mesotes*), then it can be said that this fact offers automatically to the specific soul the privilege to secure a good lot for its next life. This soul will always prefer, as stated, all kinds of extremities, both during the present reincarnation and during all the following ones.

We note that Plato insists once again that, if we develop the function of the Free Will, then this development cannot be lost under any circumstances: It will accompany our soul even in Hades, and even in the following reincarnations, as well.

The cultivation of human spirit or the full restoration of the *logistikon*, the "*technosis* of the mind" of the Aristotelian philosophers, also has the purpose of the full function of the Free Will. However, Plato would rather suggest that we cannot achieve the *technosis* of our mind without a thorough study of philosophy. We should understand that, in Plato's reality, the proper function of the Free Will is absolutely related to a "rehearsal of immortality". Because, since this improved spiritual function allows us to experience a clearly better life quality during all the following reincarnations, when complete it will lead us to full immortality.

... οὕτω γὰρ εὐδαιμονέστατος γίγνεται ἄνθρωπος.

... because in this way humans achieve the greatest happiness.

....

This happiness should be understood as extending to both the current and the following lives/reincarnations of the human soul. This is the recipe for felicity according to Plato.

What we want from our life is permanent joy and the way to acquire it. The philosopher attempts to offer us some guidelines on the topic in the Myth of Er.

In the Greek language, there is a difference in meaning between the two words that are translated as happiness, *eudaemonia* and *eutychia*. The former corresponds to a permanent state, during which humans can easily (*eu*) communicate with their *daemon* (demon), through the proper function of their Free Will; on the contrary, the latter corresponds to a momentary state, reached through the favour of luck/fortune, which naturally cannot be the case at most times in life.

....

Καὶ δὴ οὖν καὶ τότε ὁ ἐκεῖθεν ἄγγελος ἤγγελλε τὸν μὲν προφήτην οὕτως εἰπεῖν:

And at that time also the messenger from that other world reported that the prophet spoke thus:...

The messenger is the demon that accompanies Er; according to our alternative interpretation, Er himself is the one who will speak as a prophet when his soul will return to Earth, reviving his old body. Thus, his demon advises him to speak about all these experiences and topics when he returns, and in addition to complete his speech with the wise words that will follow.

The words of the demon are necessarily always "wise", since all demons communicate with God and by its very etymology the word *daemon* means the one who knows.

«Καὶ τελευταίῳ ἐπιόντι, ξὺν νῷ ἑλομένῳ,...

Even for him who comes forward last, if he make his choice wisely...

... συντόνως ζῶντι κεῖται βίος ἀγαπητός,...

... and live strenuously, there is reserved an acceptable life,...

When a certain person is at the end of his or her life and approaches the descent into Hades, if he or she have achieved the *technosis* of the mind, so that he or she is able to make wise choices, having succeeded in coordinating the inferior and the superior self while still living on Earth, then this person will enjoy a decent and even likable life during the next reincarnation. This coordination of the two "selves" is accomplished only through the cultivation of the Free Will.

... οὐ κακός.

... a life without evil.

Μήτε ὁ ἄρχων αἱρέσεως ἀμελείτω...

Neither the first one in the choice should remain without advice,...

The "life without evil" has to do with the avoidance of a bad choice of role for the next incarnation of the specific soul. The one who operates the Free Will in the proper manner is virtually impossible to choose some inadequate role. The phrase *"the first one in the choice"* can be interpreted as "the one who functions properly his Free Will".

...μήτε ὁ τελευτῶν ἀθυμείτω.»

... nor the last one [or: the dying one] should be discouraged."

The persons with a proper Free Will do not get disappointed when dying, because they know that they can choose the best roles that will secure for them a relaxed next life. Since the proper Free Will, according to Plato, is retained when we die, its conquest is a kind of initiation that corresponds to the "Descent to Hades", which reveals the proper destination of our life: the continuous improvement of the quality of our soul, until one day we will be able to reach the point of experiencing the "paradise".

The demon advises Er to reveal to humans on Earth how great is the value of initiation and the cultivation of the Free Will in the issue of the application of justice.

At this point, knowing by now enough of the secrets of the way the mechanism of reincarnations functions, the reader could understand that there are 5 entirely discrete ranks of souls, depending on the level of proper function of Free Will they managed to achieve. These are the following:

The virtuous or heroic souls, who in our astronomical analogy have succeeded in leaving our planetary system and travel to other parts of the Universe, known as the "Fortunate Isles" or the "Isles of the Blessed".

The particularly righteous souls, who through the third Van Allen Belt can reach up to the Oort cloud. These souls have passed through the meadows of Persephone and have received their lot from the knees of Lachesis.

The less righteous souls, who can reach up to the outer Van Allen belt and from there they can travel to the meadows of Persephone, which can be paralleled to the near side of the Moon; there they have also the right to choose the lot of their next reincarnation.

The unjust souls, who can ascend only to the inner Van Allen belt and from that region they get reincarnated compulsively without having the right to choose their lot.

Finally, the truly evil souls, who correspond to the worst case and are thrown into the Tartarus, imagined as a region far below the Earth, and they cannot be reincarnated again.

In other words, there are completely different movements of the souls, which depend on these five "levels of justice" to which they belong.

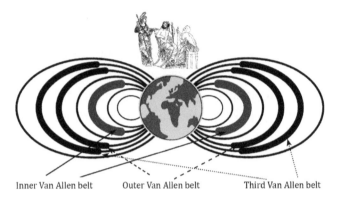

Inner Van Allen belt   Outer Van Allen belt   Third Van Allen belt

Chapter 14

THE UNIQUE VALUE OF PHILOSOPHY AND OF THE FREE WILL

Εἰπόντος δὲ ταῦτα τὸν πρῶτον λαχόντα ἔφη εὐθὺς ἐπιόντα τὴν μεγίστην τυραννίδα ἑλέσθαι, καὶ ὑπὸ ἀφροσύνης τε καὶ λαιμαργίας οὐ πάντα ἱκανῶς ἀνασκεψάμενον ἑλέσθαι, ἀλλ᾽ [619c] αὐτὸν λαθεῖν ἐνοῦσαν εἱμαρμένην παίδων αὐτοῦ βρώσεις καὶ ἄλλα κακά: ἐπειδὴ δὲ κατὰ σχολὴν σκέψασθαι, κόπτεσθαί τε καὶ ὀδύρεσθαι τὴν αἵρεσιν, οὐκ ἐμμένοντα τοῖς προρρηθεῖσιν ὑπὸ τοῦ προφήτου: οὐ γὰρ ἑαυτὸν αἰτιᾶσθαι τῶν κακῶν, ἀλλὰ τύχην τε καὶ δαίμονας καὶ πάντα μᾶλλον ἀνθ᾽ ἑαυτοῦ. εἶναι δὲ αὐτὸν τῶν ἐκ τοῦ οὐρανοῦ ἠκόντων, ἐν τεταγμένῃ πολιτείᾳ ἐν τῷ προτέρῳ βίῳ βεβιωκότα, ἔθει [619d] ἄνευ φιλοσοφίας ἀρετῆς μετειληφότα. ὡς δὲ καὶ εἰπεῖν, οὐκ ἐλάττους εἶναι ἐν τοῖς τοιούτοις ἁλισκομένους τοὺς ἐκ τοῦ οὐρανοῦ ἤκοντας, ἅτε πόνων ἀγυμνάστους: τῶν δ᾽ ἐκ τῆς γῆς τοὺς πολλούς, ἅτε αὐτούς τε πεπονηκότας ἄλλους τε ἑωρακότας, οὐκ ἐξ ἐπιδρομῆς τὰς αἱρέσεις ποιεῖσθαι. διὸ δὴ καὶ μεταβολὴν τῶν κακῶν καὶ τῶν ἀγαθῶν ταῖς πολλαῖς τῶν ψυχῶν γίγνεσθαι καὶ διὰ τὴν τοῦ κλήρου τύχην: ἐπεὶ εἴ τις ἀεί, ὁπότε εἰς τὸν ἐνθάδε βίον ἀφικνοῖτο, ὑγιῶς φιλοσοφοῖ [619e] καὶ ὁ κλῆρος αὐτῷ τῆς αἱρέσεως μὴ ἐν τελευταίοις πίπτοι, κινδυνεύει ἐκ τῶν ἐκεῖθεν ἀπαγγελλομένων οὐ μόνον

229

ἐνθάδε εὐδαιμονεῖν ἄν, ἀλλὰ καὶ τὴν ἐνθένδε ἐκεῖσε καὶ δεῦρο πάλιν πορείαν οὐκ ἂν χθονίαν καὶ τραχεῖαν πορεύεσθαι, ἀλλὰ λείαν τε καὶ οὐρανίαν.

Εἰπόντος δὲ ταῦτα τὸν πρῶτον λαχόντα ἔφη εὐθὺς ἐπιόντα τὴν μεγίστην τυραννίδα ἐλέσθαι,...

After these had been said [by the prophet or by the demon], he added that the soul who drew the first lot at once sprang to seize the greatest tyranny,...

... καὶ ὑπὸ ἀφροσύνης τε καὶ λαιμαργίας οὐ πάντα ἱκανῶς ἀνασκεψάμενον ἐλέσθαι,...

... and that in his foolishness and greed he chose it without sufficient thought and examination,...

... ἀλλ' αὐτὸν λαθεῖν ἐνοῦσαν εἱμαρμένην παίδων αὐτοῦ βρώσεις καὶ ἄλλα κακά:...

... but in doing so he failed to notice that it involved the fate of eating his own children, and other horrors;...

... ἐπειδὴ δὲ κατὰ σχολὴν σκέψασθαι,...

... and when he inspected [his future life] at leisure,...

... κόπτεσθαί τε καὶ ὀδύρεσθαι τὴν αἵρεσιν,...

... he beat his breast and bewailed his choice...

... οὐκ ἐμμένοντα τοῖς προρρηθεῖσιν ὑπὸ τοῦ προφήτου;...

... and the fact that he had not paid attention to the warning of the prophet;...

As soon as Er completed the words his demon had advised him to speak, he continued his narration by mentioning a certain soul that opened the first of the lots that were at the soul's disposal and immediately chose to adopt its role, which corresponded to a tyrant of the worst kind.

Because of the great foolishness and thirst for power of the particular soul, an appropriate lot was not selected and the events contained in that tyrant's life were not examined. This was a fatal omission, because the role included as an inescapable event for the tyrant to murder and eat his children, and to commit other, similarly heinous crimes.

And when the soul realised in time the consequences of the role so hastily selected, that same soul showed great exasperation, but no real and deep remorse, as can be seen in the following.

The souls are given the opportunity to become prophets of their next incarnated life, since before their reincarnation they have the right to examine their roles and all their consequences (end of Chapter 9); but they should be prudent enough to perceive whether the conditions of the next life satisfy them. If they do not seize this opportunity, they will probably realise in the future that they chose the wrong lot. A method for them to minimise this probability is to study philosophy during their time on Earth, in order to understand the significance and the value of Free Will, and through it to acquire the possibility to greatly improve the choice and the performance of their future roles. In other words, to take their future in their own hands, something that for Plato is the result of an exercise in philosophy.

... οὐ γὰρ ἑαυτὸν αἰτιᾶσθαι τῶν κακῶν,...

... but he did not blame himself for his woes,...

... ἀλλὰ τύχην τε καὶ δαίμονας καὶ πάντα μᾶλλον ἀνθ᾽ ἑαυτοῦ.

... but fortune and the gods and anything except himself.

....

However, if the word "himself" is taken to mean the inferior self of the soul, the representation of the embodied soul, then this soul is right; for we must not connect our inferior self with the responsibility of a bad choice. Of course, the soul is the responsible part for randomly choosing a certain role (i.e. without prior examination); and as an extension it also chose the demon associated with the particular role, plus all the connected processes. The innocent part is the inferior self, and in this way we could interpret the second phrase, as well. It goes without saying that no god can be held responsible for the bad choice, nor any demon. The real culprit is the lack of initiation of that soul.

Εἶναι δὲ αὐτὸν τῶν ἐκ τοῦ οὐρανοῦ ἡκόντων,...

Now that particular soul was one of those who had come down from heaven,...

... ἐν τεταγμένῃ πολιτείᾳ ἐν τῷ προτέρῳ βίῳ βεβιωκότα,...

... and was embodied to a man who had lived in a well-ordered, politically organised state in the former existence (reincarnation),

The demon also comes down from heaven, in order to lead the soul to the next reincarnation, if Hades can be said to be located on the Moon. Every soul will follow a life compatible with the evolution of that soul up to the specific point in time. The more evolved are the souls, the better the role they can choose for their next reincarnation. There is a question Plato seems just to touch here: whether living in a well-governed state with excellent laws can contribute to or have a positive effect on the evolution of an embodied soul.

... ἔθει ἄνευ φιλοσοφίας ἀρετῆς μετειληφότα.

... participating in virtue by being used to it and not by philosophy.

The demon also serves to prevent the soul from believing that it is possible to evolve without the aid of philosophy, even if that soul is otherwise habitually virtuous through participating in the common virtue of the society of a well-governed state.

Usually the case is that we think we can evolve our soul without dedicating some time to a thorough study of philosophy, and this is a great mistake, as Plato clearly informs us here. Philosophy is for him the only path that can lead us safely to the personal conquest of virtue. Incidentally, we live in an age when we are discouraged from studying the essence of philosophy and yet we are led to believe that we can comprehend abstract notions, such as the meaning of love.

Ὡς δὲ καὶ εἰπεῖν, οὐκ ἐλάττους εἶναι ἐν τοῖς τοιούτοις ἀλισκομένους τοὺς ἐκ τοῦ οὐρανοῦ ἥκοντας, ἅτε πόνων ἀγυμνάστους:...

And one could probably say that the majority of those who were thus spoiled (or: consumed) were of the souls that had descended from heaven, inasmuch as they were unexercised in suffering;...

Alternatively, we could theorise that most souls select as their companion a demon who do not know how to use; and in this aspect they are like humans who attempt to face hardships without being prepared accordingly. This is the result of the lack of study of philosophy. For example, we think that we have the power to love without having been interested ever to study the philosophical dimension of love.

This happens because we do not communicate with our demon, who would prevent us from such a kind of thoughtless and ultimately erroneous behaviour. As much the human body needs exercise, the human soul needs philosophy, in order to be assisted to avoid dangers arising from various hardships; for the soul can be compared to an inexperienced soldier in the case of war.

... τῶν δ' ἐκ τῆς γῆς τοὺς πολλούς, ἅτε αὐτούς τε πεπονηκότας ἄλλους τε ἐωρακότας, οὐκ ἐξ ἐπιδρομῆς τὰς αἱρέσεις ποιεῖσθαι.

... on the other hand, most of those who had ascended from the Earth, since they had themselves suffered and seen the sufferings of others, did not make their choice hastily.

We ought to know that the souls of most people on Earth have been reincarnated in order to experience in practice hard situations, while there are also some who have been reincarnated with the aim to support them. Most souls have to be punished; however, there is a minority of other souls, presumably more evolved than the former ones, who during their embodied lives are not anymore obliged to experience so difficult situations: their purpose on Earth is to stand by the struggling souls. These helpful souls possess the moral virtue of magnanimity; they face danger and trouble with tranquillity and firmness, and they disdain injustice. Yet, here we are informed that after death the punished souls have an advantage with respect to their lot choice. Every soul should known that has no reason to be in a hurry in order to choose some better role.

Διὸ δὴ καὶ μεταβολὴν τῶν κακῶν καὶ τῶν ἀγαθῶν ταῖς πολλαῖς τῶν ψυχῶν γίγνεσθαι καὶ διὰ τὴν τοῦ κλήρου τύχην:...

For which reason also takes place an interchange of good and evil for most of the souls, as well as because of the chances of the lot;...

The result of performing a favorable role and the result of performing a role that ends up becoming unfavorable depend on how the proper and suitable performance of each role will be achieved. At this point Plato hints once again at the prevailing issue of the Free Will.

... ἐπεὶ εἴ τις ἀεί, ὁπότε εἰς τὸν ἐνθάδε βίον ἀφικνοῖτο,...

... however, if a certain person each time he returned to the life of this world...

... ὑγιῶς φιλοσοφοῖ καὶ ὁ κλῆρος αὐτῷ τῆς αἱρέσεως μὴ ἐν τελευταίοις πίπτοι,...

... philosophised in a healthy way, and the lot of his

choice did not appear among the last,...

... κινδυνεύει ἐκ τῶν ἐκεῖθεν ἀπαγγελλομένων οὐ μόνον ἐνθάδε εὐδαιμονεῖν ἄν,...

... then we may risk to affirm, from what was reported thence, that not only he would be happy here,...

... ἀλλὰ καὶ τὴν ἐνθένδε ἐκεῖσε καὶ δεῦρο πάλιν πορείαν...

... but also that the path of his travel to the other side and of his return to this world...

This should take place in the case of all souls that reincarnate having achieved to adopt during their previous life or lives a philosophical way of living, irrespective of the role they have chosen for their current life. Such souls will not be harmed by any kind or type of role. In any other case, the adverse consequences of an inadequate performance of a role are not restricted to the present reincarnation, but they most probably extend to the travels of the souls outside of the body, as well as to their future reincarnations.

Here the continuity in the series of reincarnations appears clearly, together with the great importance of the evolution of the souls. Because an evolved soul can enjoy felicity not only in the present reincarnation, but also in all subsequent ones. In other words, what matters is the soul's evolution that is connected to the proper function of Free Will, not the kind of role.

It follows that we must dedicate all our powers to the advancement of the evolution of our soul as much as possible, by controlling our passions and upgrading our intellect.

... οὐκ ἂν χθονίαν καὶ τραχεῖαν πορεύεσθαι,...

... *would not be underground and rough,...*

... ἀλλὰ λείαν τε καὶ οὐρανίαν.

... *but smooth and through the heavens.*

If the souls perform their roles adequately, that is with the help of philosophy and fully exerting their Free Will, then their next reincarnations will not be rough and full of difficulties, as we learned that happens with most of the souls reincarnated on Earth; on the contrary, the integrated function of the Free Will would bring about a smooth way of living, reminiscent of a heavenly one.

Thus, the value of the proper function of our Free Will is so great that can lead us to live a heavenly life here on the Earth, reminding the phrase of the Lord's Prayer "on earth, as it is in heaven". It can be said, indeed, that Plato acts here as a "prophet" of a religion strongly upholding the Free Will; according to that religion, the proper exertion of Free Will by humans would be God's will.

Chapter 15
THE UNKNOWN SECRETS
OF METEMPSYCHOSIS
AND REINCARNATIONS

Ταύτην γὰρ δὴ ἔφη τὴν θέαν ἀξίαν εἶναι ἰδεῖν, ὡς ἕκασται
[620a] αἱ ψυχαὶ ᾑροῦντο τοὺς βίους· ἐλεινήν τε γὰρ ἰδεῖν
εἶναι καὶ γελοίαν καὶ θαυμασίαν. κατὰ συνήθειαν γὰρ τοῦ
προτέρου βίου τὰ πολλὰ αἱρεῖσθαι. ἰδεῖν μὲν γὰρ ψυχὴν
ἔφη τήν ποτε Ὀρφέως γενομένην κύκνου βίον αἱρουμένην,
μίσει τοῦ γυναικείου γένους διὰ τὸν ὑπ' ἐκείνων θάνατον
οὐκ ἐθέλουσαν ἐν γυναικὶ γεννηθεῖσαν γενέσθαι· ἰδεῖν
δὲ τὴν Θαμύρου ἀηδόνος ἑλομένην· ἰδεῖν δὲ καὶ κύκνον
μεταβάλλοντα εἰς ἀνθρωπίνου βίου αἵρεσιν, καὶ ἄλλα ζῷα
μουσικὰ ὡσαύτως. [620b] εἰκοστὴν δὲ λαχοῦσαν ψυχὴν
ἑλέσθαι λέοντος βίον· εἶναι δὲ τὴν Αἴαντος τοῦ Τελαμωνίου,
φεύγουσαν ἄνθρωπον γενέσθαι, μεμνημένην τῆς τῶν ὅπλων
κρίσεως. τὴν δ' ἐπὶ τούτῳ Ἀγαμέμνονος· ἔχθρᾳ δὲ καὶ ταύτην
τοῦ ἀνθρωπίνου γένους διὰ τὰ πάθη ἀετοῦ διαλλάξαι βίον.
ἐν μέσοις δὲ λαχοῦσαν τὴν Ἀταλάντης ψυχήν, κατιδοῦσαν
μεγάλας τιμὰς ἀθλητοῦ ἀνδρός, οὐ δύνασθαι παρελθεῖν,
ἀλλὰ λαβεῖν. μετὰ [620c] δὲ ταύτην ἰδεῖν τὴν Ἐπειοῦ τοῦ
Πανοπέως εἰς τεχνικῆς γυναικὸς ἰοῦσαν φύσιν· πόρρω δ'

ἐν ὑστάτοις ἰδεῖν τὴν τοῦ γελωτοποιοῦ Θερσίτου πίθηκον ἐνδυομένην. κατὰ τύχην δὲ τὴν Ὀδυσσέως λαχοῦσαν πασῶν ὑστάτην αἱρησομένην ἰέναι, μνήμῃ δὲ τῶν προτέρων πόνων φιλοτιμίας λελωφηκυῖαν ζητεῖν περιιοῦσαν χρόνον πολὺν βίον ἀνδρὸς ἰδιώτου ἀπράγμονος, καὶ μόγις εὑρεῖν κείμενόν που καὶ παρημελημένον [620d] ὑπὸ τῶν ἄλλων, καὶ εἰπεῖν ἰδοῦσαν ὅτι τὰ αὐτὰ ἂν ἔπραξεν καὶ πρώτη λαχοῦσα, καὶ ἀσμένην ἑλέσθαι. καὶ ἐκ τῶν ἄλλων δὴ θηρίων ὡσαύτως εἰς ἀνθρώπους ἰέναι καὶ εἰς ἄλληλα, τὰ μὲν ἄδικα εἰς τὰ ἄγρια, τὰ δὲ δίκαια εἰς τὰ ἥμερα μεταβάλλοντα, καὶ πάσας μείξεις μείγνυσθαι.

Ταύτην γὰρ δὴ ἔφη τὴν θέαν ἀξίαν εἶναι ἰδεῖν, ὡς ἕκασται αἱ ψυχαὶ ᾑροῦντο τοὺς βίους:...

[Er] said that it was a sight worth seeing to observe how the souls one by one selected their lives;...

... ἐλεινήν τε γὰρ ἰδεῖν εἶναι καὶ γελοίαν καὶ θαυμασίαν.

... it was at the same time a puzzling, pitiful, and ridiculous spectacle.

The observation of the supernatural functions pertaining to the souls, and especially of the way the souls could choose their next reincarnations, was a unique and truly worthy experience for Er. However, he immediately proceeds to characterise this procedure as pitiful and ridiculous. In addition to the selection process, the subsequent performance of each role by the respective soul can be similarly said to range from exquisite to puzzling to ridiculous. Indirectly, the author wants to repeat that, irrespective of the role we choose, we can improvise in our performance of it; however, if we have not understood the true meaning of the Free Will, or if our soul is totally unevolved, these improvisations can very easily lead to puzzling, pitiful and ridiculous final results. In a sense, Plato urges the readers to try to avoid following a way of living that humiliates and ridicules our life.

Κατὰ συνήθειαν γὰρ τοῦ προτέρου βίου τὰ πολλὰ αἱρεῖσθαι.

Because the choices the souls made were determined for the most part by the habits of their former life.

Ἰδεῖν μὲν γὰρ ψυχὴν ἔφη τήν ποτε Ὀρφέως γενομένην κύκνου βίον αἱρουμένην,...

For example, he saw the soul that once belonged to Orpheus, he said, selecting the life of a swan,...

... μίσει τοῦ γυναικείου γένους διὰ τὸν ὑπ' ἐκείνων θάνατον οὐκ ἐθέλουσαν ἐν γυναικὶ γεννηθεῖσαν γενέσθαι:...

... because from hatred of the gender of women, owing to his death by them, that soul did not want to be con-

ceived and born of a woman;...

Most role choices, according to Er, pertain to the habits of the immediately preceding life of each soul. Er proceeds to offer a number of examples of souls that used to belong to famous personalities of Greek mythology.

The first example is the soul of Orpheus, who hated women because Orpheus had been killed by women (the Thracian Maenads). Ovid writes that Orpheus *"had abstained from the love of women, either because things ended badly for him, or because he had sworn to do so"* (The Metamorphoses, Book X, trans. A.S. Kline). Orpheus became the first priest of Apollo (his brother according to some secondary traditions) and at the same time he was a musician, a poet, and a prophet. For some, while Hermes had invented the lyre, Orpheus had perfected it. With the power of his music and song, he could charm the savage animals, make trees and rocks to dance, and even stop the flow of rivers.

As one of the initiators of civilisation, Orpheus was also said to have taught to the humankind the arts of writing, of medicine and pharmaceuticals, and of agriculture, where Orpheus assumes the Eleusinian role of Triptolemus as giver of Demeter's knowledge to humanity. Closely connected with the religious life, Orpheus established several important mystic ceremonies and rituals.

Through the example of the soul of Orpheus, we realise that our soul has an additional important option, i.e. to occupy the body of another organism of the animal kingdom, and not only of a mammal, but even of a bird (metempsychosis).

Orpheus

... ἰδεῖν δὲ τὴν Θαμύρου ἀηδόνος ἑλομένην,...

... he also saw the soul of Thamyris choosing the life of a nightingale;...

Thamyris or Thamyras, according to Homer and Euripides, was also a Thracian singer, who wrote and composed the music for epic poems such as a *Theogony*, a *Cosmogony* and a *Titanomachy*. It was also believed that he was the inventor of the ancient Greek Dorian mode in music. Thamyris was a handsome young man and he excelled both as a singer and as a lyre player, an instrument he learned to play from his teacher Linus. Once, Thamyris boasted he could sing better than the Muses; he competed against them and lost, so he was punished by them with blindness and loss of the ability to make poetry and to play the lyre.

Thamyris playing his lyre

... ἰδεῖν δὲ καὶ κύκνον μεταβάλλοντα εἰς ἀνθρωπίνου βίου αἵρεσιν,...

... and on the other hand he saw a swan changing to the choice of a human life,...

The reader has to know that a soul of an animal who has preexisted as a soul of a human can choose for the next metempsychosis to return to a human existence. This selection depends on the habits the souls have acquired during their previous metempsychoses: If they have lived as humans, they can be metempsychosed to animals and then, according to their own will, they can easily return to human bodies.

However, it seems that, regarding the animals, an animal can have its soul metempsychosed into a human body for the first time not with its own will, but only according to the will of Necessity, a process that could be compared with the law of the evolution of species.

... καὶ ἄλλα ζῷα μουσικὰ ὡσαύτως.

... and similarly other animals related to the Muses.

In other words, human souls metempsychosed into various animals controlled by the Muses, could also at some point in the future be metempsychosed again into human bodies. Obviously there was the belief that the Muses had a certain function, unknown to us, in the topic of metempsychosis of human souls into animals.

Εἰκοστὴν δὲ λαχοῦσαν ψυχὴν ἑλέσθαι λέοντος βίον:...

The soul that drew the twentieth lot chose the life of a lion;...

This particular choice leads us to think that the soul in question may had been reincarnated into a body of a king in some previous human reincarnation, most probably the immediately preceding one, since the lion was from the antiquity regarded as the king of the animals.

... εἶναι δὲ τὴν Αἴαντος τοῦ Τελαμωνίου, φεύγουσαν ἄνθρωπον γενέσθαι, μεμνημένην τῆς τῶν ὅπλων κρίσεως.

> *... this was the soul of Ajax, the son of Telamon, which,*
> *because it remembered the judgement on the weapons*
> *[of Achilles], avoided becoming a human.*

The soul of Ajax could remember all too well the wrath of that king of Salamis near the end of the Trojan War, over the ownership of the armour of dead Achilles, a wrath that led Ajax to commit suicide.

Ajax was one of the suitors of Helen of Troy, so he had sworn to defend her life and honour. Consequently, he participated in the Trojan War with twelve ships and, together with Achilles and Phoenix (the son of Amyntor) was in charge of the Achaean fleet.

Homer describes Ajax as the second bravest Achaean after Achilles and stronger than Hector. Notably, Homer adds that Ajax was huge in size, a "wall of the Achaeans". He was also handsome and of a benevolent character, capable of encouraging his fellow warriors and offer advice; he even played an important role in reconciling Achilles with Agamemnon.

Under the protection of gods Hermes and Athena, Ajax carries the body of the dead Achilles back to the Greek camp. Drawing by theAntimenes Painter on an Attic black-figure neck-amphora, circa 520-510 BC.

Τὴν δ᾽ ἐπὶ τούτῳ Ἀγαμέμνονος:...

The next one was the soul of Agamemnon;...

For a similar reason the soul of Agamemnon chose to be metempsychosed into the body of an animal. Agamemnon was one of the best-known heroes of Greek mythology. He was the king of Mycenae and Argos and is considered as the most important among the leaders of the all-Greek military campaign against Troy, the Trojan War.

After his return from Troy, he was murdered by Aegisthus, the lover of his wife, Clytaemnestra, who had taken over the power in Mycenae.

The famous golden funeral mask known as "Mask of Agamemnon". It was discovered in Grave V, at the site "Grave Circle A", in Mycenae, by Heinrich Schliemann in 1876. Modern archaeological research suggests that the mask is from the 16th Century BC; it is displayed in the National Archaeological Museum of Athens.

... ἔχθρᾳ δὲ καὶ ταύτην τοῦ ἀνθρωπίνου γένους διὰ τὰ πάθη ἀετοῦ διαλλάξαι βίον.

...that soul also out of hatred of the human race because of its sufferings, exchanged its human life for that of an eagle.

Ἐν μέσοις δὲ λαχοῦσαν τὴν Ἀταλάντης ψυχήν, κατιδοῦσαν μεγάλας τιμὰς ἀθλητοῦ ἀνδρός, οὐ δύνασθαι παρελθεῖν, ἀλλὰ λαβεῖν.

Picking one of the middle lots, the soul of Atalanta

caught sight of the great honours attached to the life of a male athlete and could not pass them by, but assumed that life.

We observe that, when the soul of Atalanta, a virgin huntress renowned for her running records, happened to pick a role of a man who would be an athlete, that soul could not resist to the temptation to live again a life of athletic honours, although it belonged to the opposite sex.

At this point Plato wants to convey another important belief, which the reader of his period must had a certain difficulty to accept: Our soul, as long as "it" remains outside of a material body is neither male nor female; the soul has no sex attached to it! This is the reason that throughout this book we have avoided using the pronouns he/his or she/her when referring to a soul, although, being a personality, could neither be described with an "it". This was achieved by using always the generic plural number.

Atalanta was one of the most important "heroines" in Greek mythology and served as the only female Argonaut (according to Pseudo-Apollodorus). A Diana/Artemis-like figure, she participated in the hunt for the Calydonian Boar, managing to throw the first arrow that hit that wild beast. After the end of the Argonautic expedition, Atalanta participated in the funeral games for Pelias along with some of the most famous heroes of Greek mythology; there she defeated Peleus in wrestling, while she was also invincible as a runner.

So we realise that the soul of Atalanta, although embodied in a female body, wanted to continue to be an athlete, as being used to this occupation in the previous reincarnation, not paying the least of attention to the genre. In other words, the talents and the evolution of a given soul are not lost because of the sex chosen by that soul for the next reincarnation: they can function perfectly well in both sexes, without any problem. Even the issue of bodily strength, which is a masculine characteristic, can be resolved.

Atalanta

Μετὰ δὲ ταύτην ἰδεῖν τὴν Ἐπειοῦ τοῦ Πανοπέως εἰς τεχνικῆς γυναικὸς ἰοῦσαν φύσιν:...

After her, he saw the soul of Epeius, the son of Panopeus, entering into the nature of an arts and crafts woman;...

In addition to the example of Atalanta's soul, Plato mentions that of Epeius from the region of Phocis, the soul of whom preferred to be reincarnated as a woman.

Epeius also participated in the Trojan War and he was the

one who built the famous Trojan Horse (in Greek: *Dourian Horse* = Wooden Horse), using wood from trees cut from Ida Mountain in the region of Troy. He entered the hollow Horse together with another 29 Greek warriors and, after the Horse was pulled inside the walls of Troy by the Trojans, they conquered the city. He is also reported to participate in the funeral games conducted in the memory of Patroclus, in which he won a boxing match against Euryalus; the *Iliad* informs us that Epeius managed to throw him down with a single punch and immediately after offered him a helping hand.

... πόρρω δ' ἐν ὑστάτοις ἰδεῖν τὴν τοῦ γελωτοποιοῦ Θερσίτου πίθηκον ἐνδυομένην.

... besides that, far off in the rear he saw the soul of the buffoon Thersites transferred in the body of an ape.

Ἐν κατὰ τύχην δὲ τὴν Ὀδυσσέως λαχοῦσαν πασῶν ὑστάτην αἰρησομένην ἰέναι,...

And it happened so that the soul of Odysseus drew the last lot of all and came to make "its" choice,...

....

Odysseus (Ulysses in Latin) is the well-known mythical king of Ithaca, the basic hero of the famous epic poem Odyssey of Homer; however, *Odysseus* plays also a decisive role in the other great Homeric epic, the *Iliad*, where he distinguished himself as one of the best leaders of the Greeks and a valuable advisor to Agamemnon.

Odysseus is famous for his cleverness and ingenuity, as well as for the extremely long time he needed to return home after the Trojan War, as sung by Homer.

Odysseus as he blinds the Cyclops Polyphemus.
Greek sculpture of the 2nd Century BC.

... μνήμῃ δὲ τῶν προτέρων πόνων φιλοτιμίας λελωφηκυῖαν ζητεῖν περιοῦσαν χρόνον πολὺν βίον ἀνδρὸς ἰδιώτου ἀπράγμονος,...

... and, from memory of its former toils having rejected all ambition, went about for a long time searching for the life of a solitary citizen who minded his own business,...

... καὶ μόγις εὑρεῖν κείμενόν που καὶ παρημελημένον

ὑπὸ τῶν ἄλλων,...

... and with difficulty found one, lying in some remote place and disregarded by the others,...

... καὶ εἰπεῖν ἰδοῦσαν ὅτι τὰ αὐτὰ ἂν ἔπραξεν καὶ πρώτη λαχοῦσα, καὶ ἀσμένην ἑλέσθαι.

... and upon seeing that, [the soul of Odysseus] said that it would have done the same had it drawn the first lot, and gladly selected that life.

Καὶ ἐκ τῶν ἄλλων δὴ θηρίων ὡσαύτως εἰς ἀνθρώπους ἰέναι καὶ εἰς ἄλληλα,...

And in the same way, some of the other beasts entered into humans and into one another,...

Thus, in the next reincarnation the soul of the most famous adventurous man, Odysseus, lived a life of an anonymous person with no significant activity whatsoever. Since the soul of Odysseus, equipped with a proper function of the Free Will, was capable of interpreting correctly any role, in the new reincarnation that soul lived an insignificant yet pleasurable life. As for the souls of animals being transferred to human bodies, all this reminds us once again the theory of biological evolution.

... τὰ μὲν ἄδικα εἰς τὰ ἄγρια,...

... the unjust into wild animals,...

.... τὰ δὲ δίκαια εἰς τὰ ἥμερα μεταβάλλοντα, καὶ πάσας μείξεις μείγνυσθαι.

... the just transformed to tame, and there was every kind of mixture combined.

As a final conclusion, Plato adds that if the soul of an unjust human is metempsychosed, then that soul will enter the body of a wild beast; on the contrary, the soul of a righteous person will enter the body of a tame animal. And there are all kinds of combinations of qualities of human souls that are embodied in animals, but also of animal souls that are metempsychosed in human bodies.

Chapter 16
THE DAEMON OR GUARDIAN ANGEL
AND THE FUNCTION OF THE THREE FATES

Ἐπειδὴ δ' οὖν πάσας τὰς ψυχὰς τοὺς βίους ᾑρῆσθαι, ὥσπερ ἔλαχον ἐν τάξει προσιέναι πρὸς τὴν Λάχεσιν· ἐκείνην δ' ἐκάστῳ ὃν εἵλετο δαίμονα, τοῦτον φύλακα συμπέμπειν [620e] τοῦ βίου καὶ ἀποπληρωτὴν τῶν αἱρεθέντων. ὃν πρῶτον μὲν ἄγειν αὐτὴν πρὸς τὴν Κλωθὼ ὑπὸ τὴν ἐκείνης χεῖρά τε καὶ ἐπιστροφὴν τῆς τοῦ ἀτράκτου δίνης, κυροῦντα ἣν λαχὼν εἵλετο μοῖραν· ταύτης δ' ἐφαψάμενον αὖθις ἐπὶ τὴν τῆς Ἀτρόπου ἄγειν νῆσιν, ἀμετάστροφα τὰ ἐπικλωσθέντα ποιοῦντα· ἐντεῦθεν δὲ δὴ ἀμεταστρεπτὶ ὑπὸ τὸν τῆς [621a] ἀνάγκης ἰέναι θρόνον, καὶ δι' ἐκείνου διεξελθόντα, ἐπειδὴ καὶ οἱ ἄλλοι διῆλθον, πορεύεσθαι ἅπαντας εἰς τὸ τῆς Λήθης πεδίον διὰ καύματός τε καὶ πνίγους δεινοῦ· καὶ γὰρ εἶναι αὐτὸ κενὸν δένδρων τε καὶ ὅσα γῆ φύει. σκηνᾶσθαι οὖν σφᾶς ἤδη ἑσπέρας γιγνομένης παρὰ τὸν Ἀμέλητα ποταμόν, οὗ τὸ ὕδωρ ἀγγεῖον οὐδὲν στέγειν. μέτρον μὲν οὖν τι τοῦ ὕδατος πᾶσιν ἀναγκαῖον εἶναι πιεῖν, τοὺς δὲ φρονήσει μὴ σῳζομένους πλέον πίνειν τοῦ μέτρου· τὸν δὲ ἀεὶ πιόντα [621b] πάντων ἐπιλανθάνεσθαι. ἐπειδὴ δὲ κοιμηθῆναι καὶ μέσας νύκτας γενέσθαι, βροντήν τε καὶ σεισμὸν γενέσθαι, καὶ ἐντεῦθεν ἐξαπίνης ἄλλον ἄλλῃ φέρεσθαι ἄνω εἰς τὴν γένεσιν, ᾄττοντας ὥσπερ ἀστέρας. αὐτὸς δὲ τοῦ μὲν ὕδατος κωλυθῆναι πιεῖν: ὅπῃ μέντοι καὶ ὅπως εἰς τὸ σῶμα ἀφίκοιτο, οὐκ εἰδέναι, ἀλλ' ἐξαίφνης ἀναβλέψας ἰδεῖν ἕωθεν αὐτὸν κείμενον ἐπὶ τῇ πυρᾷ.

Ἐπειδὴ δ' οὖν πάσας τὰς ψυχὰς τοὺς βίους ᾑρῆσθαι,...

But when all the souls had chosen their lives...

... ὥσπερ ἔλαχον ἐν τάξει προσιέναι πρὸς τὴν Λάχεσιν:...

... in the order of their lots, they were marshalled and went before Lachesis;...

... ἐκείνην δ' ἑκάστῳ ὃν εἵλετο δαίμονα, τοῦτον φύλακα συμπέμπειν τοῦ βίου καὶ ἀποπληρωτὴν τῶν αἱρεθέντων.

... and she sent with each as the guardian of life and the fulfiller of the choice, the demon that the particular soul had selected.

Ὃν πρῶτον μὲν ἄγειν αὐτὴν πρὸς τὴν Κλωθὼ ὑπὸ τὴν ἐκείνης χεῖρά τε καὶ ἐπιστροφὴν τῆς τοῦ ἀτράκτου δίνης,...

And this demon led the soul first to Clotho, under her hand and her turning of the spindle,...

Having described the way all souls choose their future

reincarnations, Plato now describes the procedure followed afterwards: The souls are led before Lachesis, who assigns to each one the "guardian spirit", or demon. As a first task, the demon must lead the soul to the other Fate, Clotho, who with one hand rotates the spindle of Necessity reversely, so as to unfold the thread and thus determine the point of reincarnation in spacetime.

In other words, Lachesis is the Fate who offers to the souls the role of their next reincarnation, while Clotho is the Fate who connects each soul to the specific reincarnation, to the new "present" of that soul, by determining with precision the exact point in spacetime when the soul will be transferred to the body.

... κυροῦντα ἣν λαχὼν εἵλετο μοῖραν:...

... to ratify the destiny of his lot and choice;...

... ταύτης δ᾽ ἐφαψάμενον αὖθις ἐπὶ τὴν τῆς Ἀτρόπου ἄγειν νῆσιν,...

... and after touching her the demon again led the soul to the spinning of Atropos,...

The meaning can be here that Clotho, after rewinding the thread on the spindle of Necessity, gives the spindle to Atropos; here the mission of Clotho ends.

The reader should understand that the role chosen by the soul can correspond to any period of the past that is winded in the thread, which contains all the length and duration in spacetime of the embodied life. Plato probably believes that every soul who gets reincarnated repeats a role that has been performed by some other soul many years ago, and this decision is taken by Clotho.

Our life, hence, is compared to a real theatre, where the same role that is currently performed by us will be played in the future by other "actors" or "actresses", and most probably has also been performed in the past by someone else.

Since Clotho knows the quality of each soul, she transfers the soul to the appropriate location of spacetime, which will assist in a better performance of the specific role by the particular soul. In a sense, Clotho is the director of the play production.

... ἀμετάστροφα τὰ ἐπικλωσθέντα ποιοῦντα:...

... to render the spun thread [of the soul's destiny] irreversible;...

The souls must know that, from the moment the thread has been rewound, it is impossible for a change of destiny to be allowed.

In other words, Clotho determines the time period of the theatrical production, in which the newly reincarnated soul must appear in the role that soul has chosen. However, in this play the whole humanity is represented by souls that perform their respective roles. This is why absolutely no modification can be applied to the events that will happen during the life of the "actor" or "actress". This means that the souls have set all the future events that will take place in their reincarnated lives, without knowing them in detail beforehand.

The ancient Greek saying "*Pepromenon fygein adynaton*", "it is impossible to avoid destiny", is quite famous. Yet, at this point there is a key misunderstanding, since this is partially true. It is the destiny of the body that cannot be avoided, while the way the role of the soul is performed can be changed at any point by the particular soul. The role has to be performed, but the manner in which it will be played depends clearly on the Free Will the soul will have acquired as an acting entity. The success of the role performance is related to the degree of the soul's progress in the application of the moral virtues.

Unfortunately, humans still don't know about the uniquely important human capability of Free Will. Although we cannot avoid our destiny, that is the role we have chosen, we can greatly improve its interpretation, and hence the results will have on the evolution of our soul, depending on our philosophical standing. Then we use our Free Will properly, which means that we can even decrease the sum of the debts of our soul. Consequently, we could regard the possibility of the proper function of Free Will as the principal means for improve the destiny of our soul.

FREE WILL = The improvisations of our soul, which allow us to ameliorate the soul's destiny, regardless of how difficult that destiny is predicted to be.

... ἐντεῦθεν δὲ δὴ ἀμεταστρεπτὶ ὑπὸ τὸν τῆς ἀνάγκης ἰέναι θρόνον,...

... and then [the soul] passed irrevocably beneath the throne of Necessity,...

From this moment onwards, the soul always obeys exactly the law of Necessity or entropy, without any possibility of turning back, since being embodied, i.e. enclosed in matter, means that the soul follows the destiny and the absolute natural laws, which govern macroscopic matter, including the second law of thermodynamics.

As long as the souls remain in this region of the judges, they have the freedom to decide about the life they will choose, which means that they can operate their Free Will, ignoring the law of entropy. However, during our incarnated life, when the entropy law applies, we do not function properly our Free Will, unless we are initiated; this is the meaning of the "descent to Hades" of the Eleusinian Mysteries. The reader of the Myth of Er is at last in a position to understand the true meaning of initiation: The initiation allows us to start operating the Free Will, through which we can change the destiny of our soul!

... καὶ δι' ἐκείνου διεξελθόντα,...

... and after it passed through that,...

... ἐπειδὴ καὶ οἱ ἄλλοι διῆλθον,...

... when the others also passed,...

... πορεύεσθαι ἅπαντας εἰς τὸ τῆς Λήθης πεδίον διὰ καύματός τε καὶ πνίγους δεινοῦ:...

... they all travelled to and crossed the Plain of Oblivion, through a terrible heat and stifling atmosphere;...

After the souls pass from the previous stage, that is to say when the threads of their lives have been given to Atropos, they are led through the "oblivion region", which can be paralleled to an electromagnetic field or, better, to a region of extremely intense radiation, probably within the inner Van Allen belt. This ionising radiation erases some of their memories, which are electrically recorded.

Of course, when existing outside of a body the souls cannot drink water, since they have no body to store it. If we accept that the souls consist of electromagnetic energy, then they can affected only by electromagnetic fields. In other words, what can happen to a soul is either to retain or to lose electromagnetic recordings, exactly as a magnetic tape that can, through being magnetised or demagnetised, record new information or lose information of the past (reminiscences), respectively.

When a magnetic tape gets overwritten, traces of the previous recording that was substituted by the new one continue to exist, although they are not apparent; through a special process, they can be partially retrieved. The same can be done with the hard disks of computers.

... καὶ γὰρ εἶναι αὐτὸ κενὸν δένδρων τε καὶ ὅσα γῆ φύει.

... because it is devoid of trees and all plants.

Like seeds that have been buried under the ground (Hades) by older cultivations can germinate at some moment, under suitable conditions, similarly the memories as "seed word" remain in the state of seeds buried into a person's "unconscious", waiting for the proper conditions to "germinate", coming on the surface of consciousness.

This is the mystery of sowing and germination of memories, which was taught by Demeter (Ceres) within the frame of the Eleusinian Mysteries.

Σκηνᾶσθαι οὖν σφᾶς ἤδη ἑσπέρας γιγνομένης παρὰ τὸν Ἀμέλητα ποταμόν,...

After evening came, they camped by the Ameletas River (the "Don't Care" River),...

Metaphorically, the word *Ameletas* could be taken to mean the one who has no *melos*, i.e. musical sound, as a clarification that is has a different function from the other rivers. The verb *skenoumai*, to set tents to camp, strongly reminds the other meaning of the word *skenoma* = tent, which is the body as the bearing of the soul (mostly used by the Church Fathers). Thus it can be said that when the souls "camp" each one is actually connected with the body of an embryo, when already "evening has fallen", i.e. in the darkness of the womb.

... οὗ τὸ ὕδωρ ἀγγεῖον οὐδὲν στέγειν.

... whose water no container can hold.

Μέτρον μὲν οὖν τι τοῦ ὕδατος πᾶσιν ἀναγκαῖον εἶναι πιεῖν,...

So they were all required to drink a measured quantity of the water,...

... τοὺς δὲ φρονήσει μὴ σωζομένους πλέον πίνειν τοῦ μέτρου:...

... but those who were not saved by their prudence drank more than that specified quantity;...

....

The first phrase could also be taken to mean that the river has a continuous flow that never stops. In the metaphorical interpretation, the time the soul has to remain with the embryo in the water of the river, which can be taken to mean the amniotic fluid, until the proper time of birth will come, has to be calculated with precision. And those who do not measure this time span prudently prevent the souls from fulfilling their purpose. In other words, the moment of the childbirth does matter and the time of either natural birth or cesarean section has to be calculated, as it would not be prudent to leave these issues to luck.

.... τὸν δὲ ἀεὶ πιόντα πάντων ἐπιλανθάνεσθαι.

... and as they drank, they forgot all things.

The souls seem to undergo a double "forgetting process": first in the "Plain of Oblivion" and now by drinking the water of the river. In our metaphorical interpretation, the difference between the two processes is that the second one occurs after the reincarnation, in the embryonic phase: The embryos that "drink" the proper quantity, that is they remain in the amniotic fluid for the proper amount of time, not only forget the memories of their past lives, but also obtain the ability to learn all knowledge that is necessary to accomplish their purpose.

In other words, those who know how to calculate the proper time for the childbirth can choose the most suitable moment, a notion that reminds us of the astrological influences. An example from ancient Greek history is the legend that the mother of Alexander the Great, Olympias (actual name Myrtale) calculated the exact proper time she should deliver, so that her child would fulfil his exact destination.

Ἐπειδὴ δὲ κοιμηθῆναι καὶ μέσας νύκτας γενέσθαι,...

And after they fell asleep and the middle of the night came,...

... βροντήν τε καὶ σεισμὸν γενέσθαι,...

... there was a sound of thunder and an earthquake,...

... καὶ ἐντεῦθεν ἐξαπίνης ἄλλον ἄλλῃ φέρεσθαι ἄνω εἰς τὴν γένεσιν,...

... and they were suddenly made to float away from there, one this way, one that, upward to their birth,...

Then the souls fall asleep until they hear a sound, they wake up and, according to our interpretation, the fetus starts to move ("kick"), causing an "earthquake" in the womb. After this, the soul appears suddenly in the world with the face of a new person, "ascending" to the next stage of life, transformed from a fetus to an autonomous organism, in the sense that it can breathe, it can move freely, etc..

... ᾄττοντας ὥσπερ ἀστέρας.

... rushing like shooting stars.

The function of childbirth can be compared to a shooting

star or meteor, which remains an unseen stone (called meteoroid) until the moment it enters the atmosphere of the Earth; then, it becomes visible as a meteor, glowing from the air friction and the ionisation of the air molecules or atoms it causes.

Similarly, the fetus starts to breathe when it is released in the Earth's atmosphere; then its brain is activated and the newborn baby "shines", becoming a luminous star that traces its specific trajectory in life until getting extinguished by death.

A shooting star or meteor.

Αὐτὸς δὲ τοῦ μὲν ὕδατος κωλυθῆναι πιεῖν:...

But [Er] was not allowed to drink of the water;...

... ὅπῃ μέντοι καὶ ὅπως εἰς τὸ σῶμα ἀφίκοιτο,...

... how and in what way he returned to the body...

... οὐκ εἰδέναι,...

... he said he did not know,...

... ἀλλ' ἐξαίφνης ἀναβλέψας ἰδεῖν ἔωθεν αὐτὸν κείμενον ἐπὶ τῇ πυρᾷ.

... but suddenly recovering his [natural] vision he saw himself at dawn lying on the funeral pyre.

Chapter 17

AFTERWORD — THE SALVATION OF THE SOUL

Καὶ οὕτως, ὦ Γλαύκων, μῦθος ἐσώθη καὶ οὐκ ἀπώλετο, [621c] καὶ ἡμᾶς ἂν σώσειεν, ἂν πειθώμεθα αὐτῷ, καὶ τὸν τῆς Λήθης ποταμὸν εὖ διαβησόμεθα καὶ τὴν ψυχὴν οὐ μιανθησόμεθα. ἀλλ᾽ ἂν ἐμοὶ πειθώμεθα, νομίζοντες ἀθάνατον ψυχὴν καὶ δυνατὴν πάντα μὲν κακὰ ἀνέχεσθαι, πάντα δὲ ἀγαθά, τῆς ἄνω ὁδοῦ ἀεὶ ἑξόμεθα καὶ δικαιοσύνην μετὰ φρονήσεως παντὶ τρόπῳ ἐπιτηδεύσομεν, ἵνα καὶ ἡμῖν αὐτοῖς φίλοι ὦμεν καὶ τοῖς θεοῖς, αὐτοῦ τε μένοντες ἐνθάδε, καὶ ἐπειδὰν τὰ ἆθλα [621d] αὐτῆς κομιζώμεθα, ὥσπερ οἱ νικηφόροι περιαγειρόμενοι, καὶ ἐνθάδε καὶ ἐν τῇ χιλιέτει πορείᾳ, ἣν διεληλύθαμεν, εὖ πράττωμεν.

Καὶ οὕτως, ὦ Γλαύκων, μῦθος ἐσώθη καὶ οὐκ ἀπώλετο,...

And so, Glaucon, the tale was saved, as the saying is, and was not lost,...

... καὶ ἡμᾶς ἂν σώσειεν, ἂν πειθώμεθα αὐτῷ,...

... and it would hopefully save us if we believe it,...

The Myth was saved in the form of the above narration by Er and could help whoever listens to or reads it to save his or her soul. Plato, speaking with the mouth of Socrates, means that only if we learn all the mystic information the myth contains or hints at, and the pertaining dangers, we could save our soul, on the condition we do not think of it as a fairy tale, but instead we believe it as a reality!

... καὶ τὸν τῆς Λήθης ποταμὸν εὖ διαβησόμεθα καὶ τὴν ψυχὴν οὐ μιανθησόμεθα.

... and we will safely cross the River of Oblivion, and keep our soul unspotted from the world.

In such a case, we will be able to cross without any painful consequences and without losing all of our memories the "river of oblivion" (which is probably confused here by the author with the Plain of Oblivion, i.e. the inner Van Allen belt according to our analogy). Our soul will then be free from the ignorance and foolishness of this world.

If we believe that this myth describes the real process of reincarnation of our souls, this could probably protect us from the total elimination of the memories of previous lives caused by the "inner Van Allen belt". To lose our memories means to participate in the "ignorance" of this world, while to make a wrong paradigm selection for our next reincarnation would correspond to participating in the "foolishness" of this world.

These two behaviours of the soul compose the basic elements of the "Greek Meditation", whose sole purpose is to secure happiness in both our present and our subsequent life.

Ἀλλ᾽ ἂν ἐμοὶ πειθώμεθα, νομίζοντες ἀθάνατον ψυχὴν καὶ δυνατὴν πάντα μὲν κακὰ ἀνέχεσθαι,...

But if we are guided by me and believe that the soul is immortal and capable of enduring all evil,...

... πάντα δὲ ἀγαθά,...

... and good things,...

... τῆς ἄνω ὁδοῦ ἀεὶ ἑξόμεθα καὶ δικαιοσύνην μετὰ φρονήσεως παντὶ τρόπῳ ἐπιτηδεύσομεν,...

... then we will always keep the upward way and pursue righteousness with prudence always and in every way...

Socrates says that, if we accept what has been told and believe to the immortality of the soul, and we know that our soul has the potential, by applying "its" Free Will, to overcome all kinds of hardships, then we must understand that by properly functioning our Free Will we will acquire the ability to enjoy all spiritual goods. For in each case we will be able to follow the path that leads to the exaltation of our soul by using the virtue of prudence; and to set as an aim of our life to apply righteousness and justice in every way. Here it is indicated that prudence is the most important intellectual virtue.

... ἵνα καὶ ἡμῖν αὐτοῖς φίλοι ὦμεν καὶ τοῖς θεοῖς,...

...so that we will be dear to both ourselves and the gods,...

... αὐτοῦ τε μένοντες ἐνθάδε,...

... and both during our stay here [on Earth],...

....

As a result, we will manage at some time in the future to gain the favour of the divine entities, on the condition that we will regulate our life based on this assimilation of knowledge.

Thus, Plato makes absolutely clear that all the previous narration is not a myth, but a reality we must be acquainted with, in order to apply it in our life and thus to offer eventually to the divine entities the fruits of the virtue of prudence — for whatever we will achieve, it will have been achieved because of their assistance (of the Holy Grace in Christianity, or the three *Charites* or Graces in ancient Greek religion).

... καὶ ἐπειδὰν τὰ ἆθλα αὐτῆς κομιζώμεθα,...

... and when we receive our rewards,...

... ὥσπερ οἱ νικηφόροι περιαγειρόμενοι,...

... *as the winning athletes of the games go about [in the stadium];...*

... καὶ ἐνθάδε καὶ ἐν τῇ χιλιέτει πορείᾳ, ἣν διεληλύθαμεν,...

... *thus both here and in that voyage of a thousand years, of which I have told you,...*

... εὖ πράττωμεν.

... *we will fare well.*

If we apply prudence in our life, we will have the right to claim the respective reward and thus to be like the athletes, who, after their victory, make the "round of triumph" holding their awards over their heads. And this award will pertain not only to the present life, but also to the whole cycle of ten reincarnations we are currently in. Then and only then we will have the right to declare that at last we have fulfilled the purpose of our life!

The end purpose of our life is to win the ultimate trophy, and this aim is accomplished through acquiring the virtue of prudence and practicing righteousness/justice. This award corresponds to the proof of our salvation, integrated over the whole cycle of ten reincarnations.

Moreover, the basic prerequisite in order to be led to this

salvation is to accept that what was narrated in the Myth of Er is real and true!

As a final conclusion, we should acknowledge that, in this line of thought, the Myth of Er, from the moment it offers to us and analyses for us the method to save our soul, is probably the most important text written by Plato.

BIBLIOGRAPHY

The sources used for the philosophical part of the present book were mainly the ancient texts of Plato, Aristotle and Plutarch.

For all other information concerning ancient Greece, the 18-volume *Helios Encyclopaedic Dictionary* was used (in Greek).

For the modern scientific aspects of our interpretation, articles of the English *Wikipedia* were used as the main source. These connections of Greek philosophy with Greek mythology and modern science, especially astronomy, are an effort to restore a realistic alternative interpretation of the Platonic work, as understood by the author.

In Greek:

Helios Encyclopaedic Dictionary (*Helios* revue publ., Athens 1945-1960)

Charalampidis, G.: *Aristotelis*, Oselotos publ., Athens 2012

Charalampidis, G.: *Aristotelous Peri mnimis kai anamniseos*, Oselotos publ., Athens 2011

Charalampidis, G.: *Pythagoras, o protos philosophos*, Oselotos publ., Athens 2013

Dimitrakos, D.: *Neon Orthographikon Ermineutikon Lex-*

ikon, Yovanis publ., Athens 1969

In English:

Aristotle: *Metaphysics*. Transl. H. Tredennick. 2 vols., Loeb Classical Library 271, 287. Harvard U. Press, 1933-35

Crisp, Roger: *Aristotle: Nicomachean Ethics*. Cambridge University Press, 2000

Liddell, H.G. & Scott, R.: *A Greek–English Lexicon*, 8th ed., American Book Comp., 1901

Plato: *Plato's Republic*. Transl. by Paul Shorey (1935), annotated text @ Perseus Project

Plato: *Plato in Twelve Volumes*, transl. by H.N. Fowler. London, W Heinemann Ltd., 1925 (the dialogues *Phakjvvczaslkjggfdsavcxzz\edrus, Phaedo, Philebus, Symposium, Timaeus,* and *Meno*)

Plutarch: *Moralia*. Transl. by A.R. Shilleto, London: George Bell & Sons, 1898 (the essays "On the Face Which Appears in the Orb of the Moon", "On the Delays of Divine Vengeance" and "On the Sign of Socrates")

About the author

George A. Charalampidis was born in Thessaloniki Greece in 1969. He studied Greek Civilization, at the Faculty of Humanitarian Studies of the Greek Open University and is a member of the Aristotelian Club of Athens. From a very young age he showed an active interest and love for the teachings of ancient Greek Philosopher' s by attending many specialized courses and having as a goal to harmonize his life with the Greek ideals and achievement of "EY ZHN" (good living). In his personal life, he is engaged in research and primary translation of Aristotle's ancient texts.

He has published five books, while he writes articles in relevant journals and gives lectures and seminars, presenting the results of long personal research.

e-mail: georgiocharalampidis@gmail.com

website: www.georgecharalampidis.gr

Made in United States
North Haven, CT
01 April 2022

17774891R00153